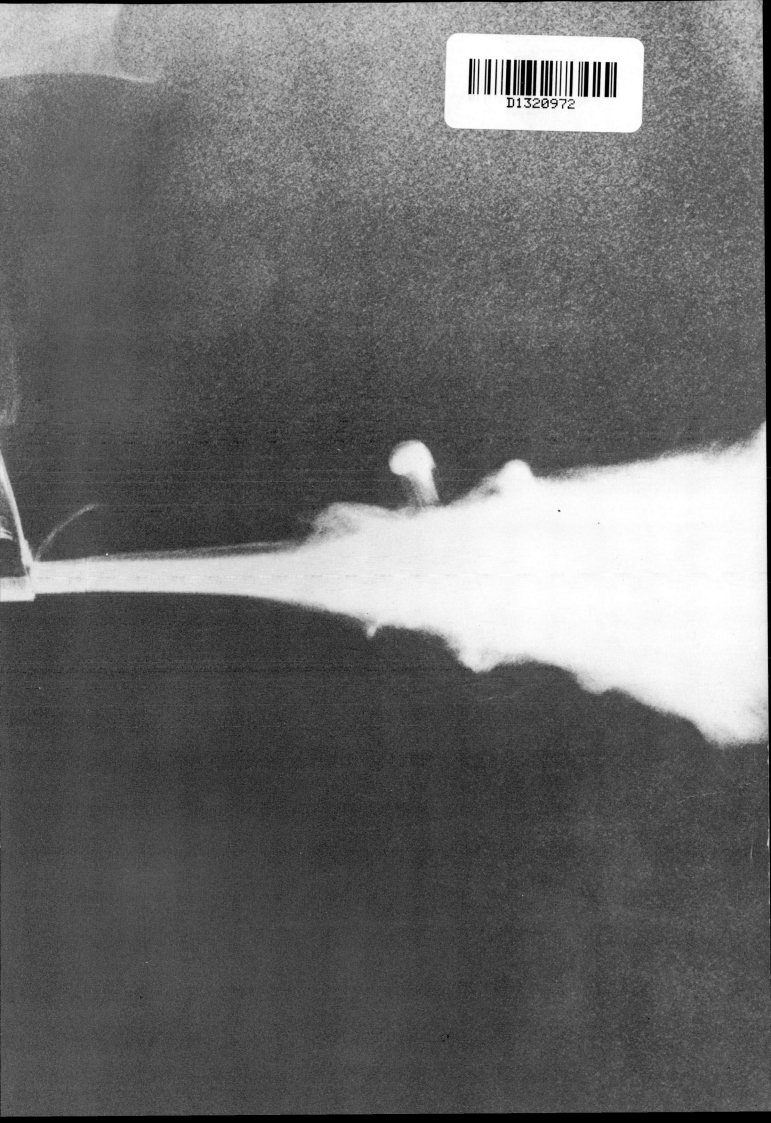

The book of SLEUTHS

Janet Pate

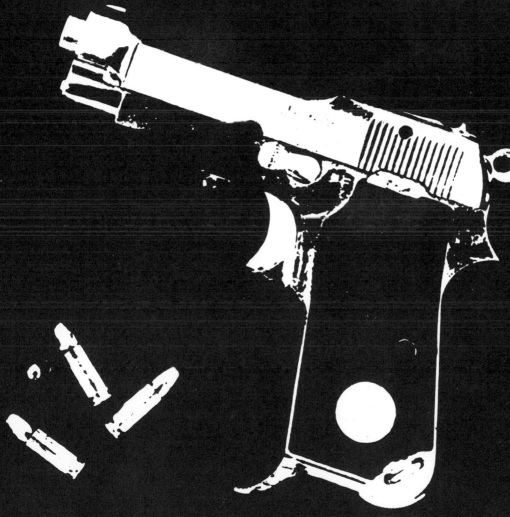

NEW ENGLISH LIBRARY

TIMES MIRROR

First published in Great Britain by
New English Library,
Barnard's Inn, Holborn, London EC1N 2JR in 1977

A *Webb&Bower* Book
Edited, designed and produced by
Webb & Bower Limited,
Exeter, England

Picture Research by Anne-Marie Ehrlich

Printed and bound in Great Britain by
Hazell Watson and Viney Limited,
Aylesbury, Buckinghamshire

450030830

Contents

Acknowledgements

Thanks are due to the following for giving their permission to quote from the works listed below:
Baskerville Investments, *A Study in Scarlet* and *Memories and Adventures* by Sir Arthur Conan Doyle; Miss D. E. Collins and Cassell, *The Father Brown Stories* by G. K. Chesterton; Miss D. E. Collins and Hutchinson, the autobiography of G. K. Chesterton; the estate of E. C. Bentley, *Trent's Last Case* by E. C. Bentley; the estate of H. C. McNeile and Hodder & Stoughton, *Bulldog Drummond* by Sapper; Hughes Massie, *The Mysterious Affair at Styles*, *The Murder on the Links*, *Curtain* and *The Body in the Library* by Agatha Christie; David Highams and Victor Gollancz, *Whose Body?* and *Five Red Herrings* by Dorothy L. Sayers; the estate of Edgar Wallace and White Lion Publishing, *The Mind of J. G. Reeder* and *Red Aces* by Edgar Wallace; Leslie Charteris and Hodder & Stoughton, *Meet the Tiger* and *Ace of Knaves* by Leslie Charteris; John Farquarson, *The Roman Hat Mystery* and *The Spanish Cape Mystery* by Ellery Queen, and *The Case of the Sulky Girl* by Erle Stanley Gardner; George Harrap, *The House without a Key* and *Charlie Chan Carries On* by Earl Derr Biggers, and *The Case of the Lucky Legs* by Erle Stanley Gardner; Georges Simenon, *Maigret and the Enigmatic Lett* by Georges Simenon; Lynette Howis, literary agent to the late John Creasey, *Introducing the Toff*, *The Toff and the Sleepy Cowboy* and *Gideon's Week* by John Creasey; Messrs Curtis Brown, *Fer-de-Lance* and *The League of Frightened Men* by Rex Stout; for publication and all other rights turn to Elizabeth Marton, 96 Fifth Avenue, New York, NY 10011 and Messrs Curtis Brown, *The Bishop Murder Case* and *Twenty Rules for Writing Detective Novels* by S. S. Van Dine; Messrs William Collins, *Dangerous Curves* by Peter Cheyney; the Helga Greene Literary Agency, *The Big Sleep* and *Raymond Chandler Speaking* by Raymond Chandler; A. D. Peters, *An Inspector Calls* by J. B. Priestley, and *The Thin Man* and *The Maltese Falcon* by Dashiell Hammett; Messrs E. P. Dutton, *My Gun Is Quick* by Mickey Spillane (1950 copyright E. P. Dutton) and *The Girl Hunters* by Mickey Spillane (1962 copyright Mickey Spillane); Messrs Hamish Hamilton and Harper & Row, *Over the High Side* by Nicolas Freeling; Ernest Tidyman, *Shaft* by Ernest Tidyman; Clive Goodwin Associates, *Gumshoe* by Neville Smith; and MCA Universal for permission to quote from *Requiem for a Cop* by Victor B. Miller.

The author would particularly like to thank the following for their help in the preparation of this book: the staff of the British Film Institute who were helpful, efficient and unfailingly cheerful; Mary V. Kelly of King Features and Lois Adams of Pocket Books who supplied me with invaluable material for *Rip Kirby* and *Kojak*; Ernest Tidyman for his advice on *Shaft*; Piers Dudgeon of Star Books who very kindly gave me a pre-publication copy of *Requiem for a Cop*; Weidenfeld & Nicolson who lent me their own edition of *The Last Shaft*; Miss Blackborow of Hughes Massie who patiently sorted through dozens of Agatha Christie titles for me; the staffs of the American Library at the University of London and the Science Museum, Kensington, for their valuable assistance; my father, Kenneth Pate, for his hard work on behalf of this book; and the gentlemen of New Scotland Yard who were always willing to help me with my enquiries.

Illustration credits
BBC copyright: 45t, 49, 86; British Library: 73, 76, 90; Commissioner of Police: 111; Courtesy of Tandem Books Ltd: 24; John R. Freeman: 9tlr, 10, 14, 15tb, 17, 18, 23, 31; King Features Syndicate: 107; Kobal Collection: 40–41, 101, 108–9; Raymond Mander and Joe Mitchenson Theatre Collection: 9bl, 15b, 30, 48, 68, 83t, 97t; Metro-Goldwyn Mayer Pictures Ltd: 42, 43; National Film Archive: 10, 11, 13, 25, 27, 29, 37, 45m, 45bl, 50, 53, 55, 56, 57, 58, 61, 63, 66, 67, 69, 70, 71tb, 74, 75, 79, 80, 81, 82, 85, 88–9, 92–3, 94–5, 97b, 98–9, 103mblr, 105, 112, 116, 117, 118–19, 120–21, 123; National Periodical Publications: 78; Robert Penn: 9; Thames Television: 114–15.

The first fictional sleuth, the Chevalier Dupin, created by Edgar Allan Poe. Illustration for *The Purloined Letter* by Frederick Simpson Coburn (1902)

Sherlock Holmes (Robert Stephens) and Dr Watson (Colin Blakely). From *The Private Life of Sherlock Holmes* (United Artists, 1970)

When an American, Edgar Allan Poe, wrote the first detective story, he set it in France where, in 1817, the Paris Sûreté had been one of the earliest-established police forces. His own country was still very young and it was to be several years before a recognized police force was formed there. America, however, was to become one of the most prolific producers of crime fiction, so perhaps it is fitting that an American should have started it all.

Victorian England was the age of gaslight, fog and narrow streets – all of which assisted the criminal. The Metropolitan Police Force was still a new concept, and officers of the law were known as 'Peelers'. Charles Dickens, at this time in the early days of his success, observed and exposed through his books the wretched conditions that bred the 'criminal classes'. It was only a year before Marshalsea, the debtors' prison, was pulled down but forty years before the notorious Newgate prison was closed.

Before World War I broke out, the enormous strides forward made in technology had revolutionized police work. The telephone, motor car, telegraphy, fingerprinting, wireless and electric light (particularly in the streets) helped to improve the detective's lot. Meanwhile some of these innovations were also making life easier for the criminal.

The writers of crime observed and recorded it all. Sexton Blake acquired a (relatively) fast car and a biplane, and Father Brown and Philip Trent put the telephone and telegram service to good use. What couldn't Inspector Bucket have achieved with a car or Sherlock Holmes with a helicopter? M. Lecoq would have gloried in the development of forensic science. But would the ingenuity of Poe, Gaboriau, Doyle and the others have been stretched to such a degree if their world had contained modern gadgets? And would the results have been so intriguing?

William Gillette as Sherlock Holmes. The Lyceum Theatre, London (1901)

Sexton Blake. An action packed illustration from *The Penny Popular* (1915)

The Chevalier C. Auguste Dupin

From **The Murders in the Rue Morgue; The Mystery of Marie Roget; The Purloined Letter** By **Edgar Allan Poe**

At such times I could not help remarking and admiring (although from his rich ideality I had been prepared to expect it) a peculiar analytic ability in Dupin. . . . His manner at these moments was frigid and abstract, his eyes were vacant in expression; while his voice, usually a rich tenor, rose into a treble, which would have sounded petulantly but for the deliberateness and entire distinctness of the enunciation. Observing him in these moods, I often dwelt meditatively upon the old philosophy of the Bi-Part Soul, and amused myself with the fancy of a double Dupin – the creative and the resolvent.

Edgar Allan Poe, *The Murders in the Rue Morgue*

The Murders in the Rue Morgue illustrated by Vierge

Born into an illustrious family but impoverished through a series of unfortunate events, Dupin lives as a recluse in Paris. Through the good grace of his creditors he is able to exist on the remnants of his inheritance and rigorous economies allow him to indulge his one passion, books.

In an obscure bookshop in the Rue Montmartre he befriends his future chronicler who, finding himself better placed than Dupin, rents and furnishes a large and desolate old house for the two friends to share in the Faubourg St Germain. Both have the same solitary temperament. During the day they are shuttered in the old house, reading, writing and conversing, emerging only at night into the outside world.

Dupin possesses an intriguing mental dexterity. Through a process of deduction, amazing in its simplicity once it is explained, he can trace to its source the development of an incident or another's train of thought. Thus he is able to explain the seemingly inexplicable. It is because of this talent that his assistance is sought by the *gendarmerie* in their not infrequent moments of perplexity.

The first of Dupin's cases to be chronicled is known as *The Murders in the Rue Morgue*. The mutilated bodies of Madame L'Espanaye and her daughter are found in their house in the Rue Morgue. Madame L'Espanaye's corpse is lying on a paved court at the rear of the building. Her daughter's body is wedged, head downwards, up the chimney of a room in which the windows are nailed down and the door has been inexplicably locked from the inside. Dupin's clever examination reveals that one of the 'nailed-down' windows is in fact worked by a spring mechanism. Continuing with his singular methods of detection he tracks down the 'murderer' – an orang-outang which has escaped from its sailor master.

After his success with the Rue Morgue case Dupin returns to the seclusion of his old life, although his help is often reluctantly sought by the Parisian police. Only two other cases are recorded. Two years after *The Murders in the Rue Morgue*, in *The Mystery of Marie Roget*, Dupin brings to justice the murderer of Marie Roget, a pretty girl of uncertain reputation. Some years after this, in *The Purloined Letter*, a letter stolen for the purposes of political blackmail is retrieved by Dupin and returned to its rightful owner.

In 1841, twelve years after Peel's Metropolitan Police Act had been passed in England, twenty-four years after the establishment of the

Surêté in France and fifty-seven years before the founding of the police force in America, Edgar Allan Poe created the Chevalier Auguste Dupin and started a new literary genre – the detective story.

Poe was born in Boston, Massachusetts, on 19 January 1809, the son of actress Elizabeth Arnold and her second husband, David Poe, Jun. Orphaned at the age of six he was brought up by John Allan, a wealthy merchant from Richmond, Virginia, with whom he later quarrelled bitterly. For a time he lived with his aunt, Mrs William Clemm, who in 1836 arranged for his marriage to her thirteen-year-old daughter, Virginia. Virginia, a gentle pretty girl, died of tuberculosis in 1847.

For most of his life Poe's gambling debts kept him poor. His ill health, both physical and mental, was aggravated by frequent bouts of drunkenness. The black depressions into which he was so often plunged increased until his sanity finally began to break. In 1849 he was found unconscious in a Baltimore street (stories of his being drunk have since been refuted) and taken to the Washington hospital where he died of exposure.

During his life he was editor of several periodicals and gained the reputation of being a brilliant critic, but he is remembered for his poems and tales – many of which reflect the dark recesses of his own mind – and as the originator of the analytical detective story. It is thought that Dupin is a projection of Poe's own personality. While he himself clung desperately to his sanity, perhaps he wished to identify with a character whose intellect and powers of rationalization excluded all emotion. In 1879 a letter was published in the New York *World*. It was signed F. D. C. and the correspondent claimed to have told Poe about a C. Auguste Dupont, a man of great analytical powers who sometimes helped the Parisian police, and that Poe subsequently modelled Dupin on him. It has also been suggested that Dupin was based on the famous French police officer, Vidocq.

The source of Poe's ingenious creation may be uncertain, but there is no doubt that Dupin, the first of all fictional detectives, has himself served as a basis for many of his successors. Surely his influence can be most keenly felt in a character created forty-six years later and who was destined to become 'immortal' – Sir Arthur Conan Doyle's Sherlock Holmes.

Leon Waycoff as Dupin with Bert Roach in *The Murders in the Rue Morgue* **(Universal, 1932)**

Publications and Performances

First publications

The Murders in the Rue Morgue. First appeared in *Graham's Magazine* in April 1841; first published in book form in 1843, *Prose Romances of E. A. Poe* (containing *The Murders in the Rue Morgue* and *The Man That Was Used Up*), Philadelphia: Wm H. Graham; *The Mystery of Marie Roget* (subtitled 'A Sequel to *The Murders in the Rue Morgue*'). First appeared in *Snowdon's Lady's Companion*, November 1842–February 1843, and *The Purloined Letter* in *Chamber's Edinburgh Journal*, November 1844, and *Gift Annual*, Philadelphia: December 1845; the first book to contain all three stories was *Tales of Edgar Allan Poe*, New York: Wiley and Putnam, 1845.

Selected published texts

The Works of the Late Edgar Allan Poe, eds R. W. Griswold, N. P. Willie and T. R. Lowell (in 2 vols). Vol I, *The Tales*, New York: Redfield, 1850. Vol II, *The Poems*, New York: Redfield, 1850.

Tales of Mystery, Imagination and Humour. The Parlour Bookcase, New York: Simms and McIntyre, 1852; London: H. Vizetelly, 1852; Routledge's Sixpenny Novels, London: G. Routledge, 1882.

The Murders in the Rue Morgue, and other Tales of Mystery. London: Sampson, Low, 1893.

The Murders in the Rue Morgue. Facsimile of the MS in the Drexel Institute, Philadelphia: G. Barrie, 1895.

The Gold Bug, The Purloined Letter and other Tales. Ed W. P. Trent, Riverside Literature Series, 1898.

The Mystery of Marie Roget. With historical and critical comments by Henry Austin, New York: R. F. Fenno, 1899.

Monsieur Dupin, the Detective Tales of Edgar Allan Poe. Illus Charles Raymond Macauley, New York: McClure Phillips, 1904.

The Purloined Letter, and other Tales. Holerth Library, Holerth Press, 1924.

The Purloined Letter. Limited edition of 250 copies, printed at The Fanfare Press, London: Ulysses Bookshop, 1931.

Tales of Mystery and Imagination. Illus Arthur Rackham, London: G. G. Harrap, 1935; New York: J. B. Lippincott, 1935.

The Purloined Letter, Berenice, and The Cask of Amontillado. Polybooks, London: Todd Publishing, 1943.

The Murders in the Rue Morgue. Polybooks, London: Todd Publishing, 1943.

Tales of Mystery and Imagination. Reprint of World's Classic Edition 1902, Oxford University Press, 1956.

Tales of Mystery and Imagination. With monotypes by M. Ayrton, London: Folio Society, 1957.

Tales of Mystery and Imagination, London: Pan Books, 1960.

Tales of Mystery and Imagination. Retold by M. W. Thomas, illus Robert Broomfield, Streamline Books, London: T. Nelson, 1966.

Tales of Mystery and Imagination. Illus Harry Clarke, London: Minerva Press, 1971.

Complete Tales and Poems of Edgar Allan Poe. New York: Vintage Books, 1975.

On film

The Murders in the Rue Morgue. Sol. A. Rosenberg Productions, 1914.

The Murders in the Rue Morgue. Universal Pictures, 1932. Leon Waycoff as Pierre Dupin.

The Mystery of Marie Roget. Universal Pictures, 1942. Patric Knowles as Chief Police Medical Officer Dupin.

Phantom of the Rue Morgue. Warner Bros (3D), 1954. Steve Forrest as Professor Paul Dupin.

No instances have been recorded of either theatre or television productions of *The Murders in the Rue Morgue, The Mystery of Marie Roget* or *The Purloined Letter.*

Leon Waycoff (left) with Bert Roach in *The Murders in the Rue Morgue* (Universal, 1932)

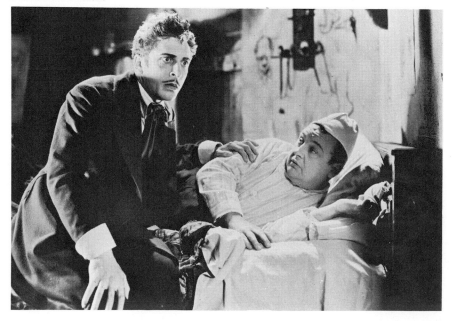

Sexton Blake

From An Original Story in the Boys' Paper The Halfpenny Marvel, 1893 By Hal Meredith

Sexton Blake belonged to the new order of detectives. He possessed a highly cultivated mind which helped to support his active courage. His refined, clean shaven face readily lent itself to any disguise, and his mobile features assisted to clinch any facial illusions he desired to produce.

Hal Meredith, The Halfpenny Marvel, 1893

Blake is a man in the prime of life and just six feet in height, with a spare athletic figure and a lean and somewhat ascetic face whose seriousness is often belied by his quick, spontaneous smile. One's impression is of an acute intelligence allied with human kindliness, and of bodily strength and will-power held easily in control. His grey eyes are his most noticeable feature, steady, level, dominating, piercing, but with a hint of humour ever lurking there.

The Sexton Blake Annual, 1936

George Curzon (right) as Sexton Blake with Harold Hallam in *Sexton Blake and the Hooded Terror* (MGM, 1938)

After taking his medical degree, Sexton Blake finds himself drawn to the science of criminology. He abandons his plans to become a doctor and sets up in business as a detective in an office in New Inn Chambers. After collaborating with the Parisian detective, Jules Gervaise, the two become partners.

Blake is an expert in boxing, ju-jutsu and marksmanship, and his chemical researches into fingerprints, bloodstains, poisons, hairs and so on have contributed much to the scientific knowledge of criminology.

After a few years Blake moves to the north end of Baker Street where his landlady, Mrs Bardell, feeds and looks after him. His suite of rooms includes a consulting room and a well-equipped laboratory. He also acquires an assistant, a large car, a bloodhound called Pedro, and a monoplane (a grey Panther with a Gnome engine, designed and built by Blake himself). He smokes a briar pipe and wears a dressing-gown when working at home.

His assistant is Edward Carter, known as Tinker. Tinker, an orphaned Cockney paperboy, helped Blake during a case. Impressed by the lad's above-average intelligence, Blake makes him his assistant. Tinker becomes the detective's indispensable right-hand man.

When reports of Sexton Blake's 'death' appear in the Press, letters and telegrams of consternation pour into editorial offices all over the country. Luckily, however, he makes a dramatic recovery when a dose of the newly discovered heart stimulant, adrenalin, is administered.

In the late fifties Blake and Tinker move to more streamlined offices in Berkeley Square. Blake wears a Luger strapped under his jacket and carries a special licence to use it, signed by the Commissioner of the Metropolitan Police. Now known as Sexton Blake Investigations, the staff is expanded to include 'pretty' Marian Lang, 'curvaceous' Louise Pringle and 'beautiful' Paula Dane.

Cover of a 1915 edition of *The Sexton Blake Library*

Sexton Blake first appeared in a modest story by Hal Meredith in the boys' paper *The Halfpenny Marvel* in 1893. His image was, to say the least, underdeveloped – he played second fiddle in a plot involving the kidnapping of an aristocratic changeling. After a couple of desultory appearances in *The Halfpenny Marvel* he was featured in another boys' weekly paper *The Union Jack*. Still he proved slow to take off and was abandoned for a short while then brought out again, dusted down, taken away from the Inns of Court and rehoused in Baker Street apartments with the addition of an assistant, a dog and a landlady. The Baker Street address, the scientific experiments, the briar pipe and the dressing-gown may have depressed the Holmesian ghost but it delighted millions of readers. In 1915 the first of the 'Sexton Blake Library' was published and this continued into the sixties. *The Union Jack* printed Blake stories for thirty-nine years until it was renamed *Detective Weekly* in 1933, with Sexton Blake as the main feature. He also made guest appearances in other periodicals.

As the times changed so did Blake. Gradually he acquired the most modern of gadgets – a car, an aeroplane and so on. In the late 1950s echoes of Holmes were dissolving into echoes of Bond. Blake now wore a Luger strapped under his jacket, the clip joint replaced the opium den, and three sexy girls replaced Mrs Bardell. But the Sexton Blake of yesteryear did not vanish entirely. In *The Savage Squeeze*, 1965, Blake tracks his suspect to a strip club, but loses him in the general exodus at the end of the show, for, unlike the uncouth masses, Blake stands to attention while the strip-club band plays the national anthem!

Illustrations for Sexton Blake. *The Penny Popular*, 1915

Sexton Blake's bloodhound Pedro. A member of the cast on tour with a production of *Sexton Blake, Detective* **(1910)**

Publications and Performances

Published texts

The Halfpenny Marvel. Fleetway Publications, 1893.

The Union Jack. Fleetway Publications, 1894.

'The Sexton Blake Library'. Amalgamated Press, 1915–59.

Detective Weekly. Fleetway Publications, 1933.

The Sexton Blake Annual. Fleetway Publications, 1938.

'Sexton Blake Library'. Mayflower-Dell Publications, 1959–63.

On film

The Stolen Heirlooms. Walturdaw Productions, 1915. Henry Lorraine as Sexton Blake.

Sexton Blake and the Bearded Doctor, 1935; *Sexton Blake and the Mademoiselle*, 1935; *Sexton Blake and the Hooded Terror*, 1938. MGM/Fox. George Curzon as Sexton Blake.

Meet Sexton Blake, The Echo Murders. British National, 1944. David Farrar as Sexton Blake.

Murder at Site Three. Francis Tearle Productions, 1959. Geoffrey Toone as Sexton Blake.

Television

Sexton Blake (series). Associated Rediffusion, 1967–8. Laurence Payne as Sexton Blake.

In the theatre

Sexton Blake by C. Douglas Carlile, 1907. Surrey Theatre.

Sexton Blake, Detective. Produced by J. M. East, 1908. Horace Hunter as Sexton Blake.

February	Crown Theatre, Peckham
March	West London Theatre
April	Shakespeare Theatre, Clapham Junction
April	Theatre Royal, Woolwich
May	Dalston Theatre
May	County Theatre, Kingston
November	Theatre Royal, Stratford East

Sexton Blake on the East Coast. A detective sketch in three scenes by J. Russell Bogue, 1915. Camberwell Palace. James Duncan as Sexton Blake.

Sexton Blake by Donald Stuart, 1936. Prince Edward Theatre. Arthur Wontner as Sexton Blake.

Ralph Henderson

From **The Notting Hill Mystery** By **Charles Felix**

Mr. Ralph Henderson to
the Secretary of the
Life Assurance Society

Private Enquiry Office
Clement's Inn
17th Jan. 1858

Gentlemen,

In laying before you the extraordinary revelations arising from my examination into the case of the late Madame R——, I have to apologise for the delay in carrying out your instructions of November last. It has been occasioned, not by neglect on my part, but by the unexpected extent of intricacy of the inquiry into which I have been led. I confess that after this minute and laborious investigation I could still have wished a more satisfactory result, but a perusal of the accompanying documents, on the accuracy and completeness of which you may fully rely, will no doubt not satisfy you of the unusual difficulty of the case.

Charles Felix, *The Notting Hill Mystery*

Very little is known of Ralph Henderson, except that he had a private enquiry office in Clement's Inn, London, and only one of his cases has been brought to the public notice. His findings in this instance were, however, of such a startling nature that they attracted much attention on publication after his death. Mr Henderson had investigated the death of Madame R—— on behalf of life-assurance associations in London, Manchester, Liverpool, Edinburgh and Dublin where Baron R—— had placed policies on his wife, each one for £500, the maximum amount permitted in each office. Letters from Mr Henderson and others, together with signed statements from witnesses involved in his investigation, were collected by Charles Felix and published after Henderson's death. They revealed how Henderson extended his researches to another and most singular case which he believed to be connected with his own enquiries, providing a strange solution to both mysteries.

The following tale was first presented to the public in 1862. In 1832 a Sir Edward Boleton of Beechwood, Kent, was killed in a duel. His wife consequently died while giving birth to twin girls. The children, Gertrude and Catherine, were both frail and of a nervous temperament and it was noticed that if one twin was ill a sympathy caused the other to suffer the same symptoms. They were given into the care of a poor but honest woman, Sarah Taylor, of Hastings. During a picnic outing in 1837 Catherine disappeared and after every effort had been made to trace her it was concluded that she had been kidnapped by a gang of gipsies.

In 1851 Gertrude married William Anderton. The couple were devoted and it was a happy marriage marred only by the ill health from which both suffered. They were persuaded to try mesmerism as a remedy. This proved helpful to Mrs Anderton but not her husband who discontinued his treatment. Mrs Anderton became the patient of Baron R—— who influenced her through a medium, 'Rosalie'. 'Rosalie' was of similar build to Mrs Anderton and although she was not able to speak English, an instant and unusually strong sympathy was established between the two women. After the baron and 'Rosalie' left London Mrs Anderton was stricken with what appeared to be antimonial poisoning from which she died in extreme agony. Although no poison was found in her body her husband was suspected of murder and was driven to suicide.

It was at this time that the baron's wife suffered a severe bout of antimonial poisoning from which she recovered. Sometime later, however, while supposedly walking in her sleep, she swallowed some acid from her husband's private laboratory and died.

The letters collected by Mr Henderson are evidence to his belief that the medium, 'Rosalie', was Mrs Anderton's twin. Mr Anderton had innocently told the baron of his wife's past history. The baron guessed the women's relationship, and after some secret investigations had ascertained that a large legacy would be due to Mr Anderton on the death of his wife and her sister (should she be traced) if they both died without issue. The baron married 'Rosalie' and poisoned her. Although she survived, Mrs Anderton, through the strange sympathy of the twins, died. After urging Anderton to suicide he mesmerized his wife and compelled her to swallow acid. This left him the sole heir to the legacy.

Mr Henderson's report concludes with his own summing-up of the case. We are not told whether Baron R—— was brought to trial in the light of his disclosures. But it was thought that Mr Henderson had discovered an exceptionally bizarre crime.

The appearance of 'The Notting Hill Mystery' in the magazine *Once a Week* in 1862 marked a turning-point in detective fiction. Until then it had consisted only of short stories. With 'The Notting Hill Mystery', *Once a Week* presented its readers with a full-length novel in serial form relating the investigations of a private detective, Ralph Henderson, into an intricate case using the evidence of letters and diaries, a method used later by Wilkie Collins with *The Moonstone* and Bram Stoker with *Dracula*.

This bland and slightly distant manner of story telling had the effect of highlighting the bizarre and horrific aspects of the plot. The Victorians enjoyed their bit of horror as much as they enjoyed their moments of sweetness and 'The Notting Hill Mystery' was a huge success. It was put into book form after which it faded into obscurity.

Publications

Published texts

'The Notting Hill Mystery' was first published in the magazine *Once a Week* in eight instalments from November 1862 to January 1863, published London: Bradbury & Evans; published in book form in 1865, London: Saunders, Otley & Co; reappeared in *Novels of Mystery from the Victorian Age* (containing 'The Notting Hill Mystery', 'Dr Jekyll and Mr Hyde', 'Carmilla' and 'The Woman in White'), London: Pilot Press, 1945.

There is no record of a theatre or film production of *The Notting Hill Mystery*.

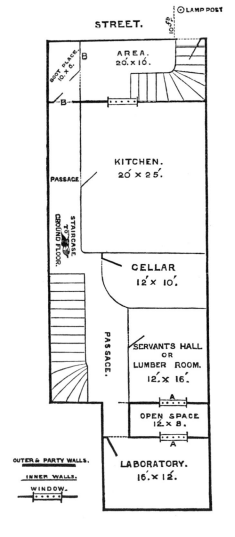

Plan of Baron R——'s basement. *The Notting Hill Mystery* **was the first crime story in which diagrams were used**

Monsieur Lecoq

From **Monsieur Lecoq, Le Crime D'Orcival (Crime at Orcival);
Le Dossier 113 (File no 113); L'Affaire LeRouge (The Widow LeRouge)**
By **Emile Gaboriau**

He took off his stiff cravat and gold spectacles, and removed the
close wig from his thick black hair. The official Lecoq had disappeared, leaving in his place the genuine Lecoq whom nobody
knew – a good-looking young man, with a bold, determined manner, and brilliant, piercing eyes. But he only remained himself for an
instant. Seated before a dressing-table covered with more cosmetics,
paints, perfumes, false hair, and other shams than are to be found
on the toilet-tables of our modern belles, he began to undo the work
of nature and to make himself a new face. He worked slowly,
handling his brushes with great care. But in an hour he had ac-
complished one of his daily masterpieces. When he had finished, he
was no longer Lecoq: he was the stout gentleman with red whiskers,
whom Fanferlot had failed to recognize.

Emile Gaboriau, *Le Dossier 113*

Cover illustration for an English version of
The Mystery of Orcival, **1887**

Lecoq is the well-educated son of a wealthy respectable Normandy
family. While he is in Paris studying law both his parents die and he
learns that his father was financially ruined. He is left destitute and
soon finds that academic achievement is little use in the fight for
survival. He earns a living as best he can in a variety of jobs and after
a while is employed by Baron Moser, a well-known astronomer. For
a 100 francs a month he spends his days solving complicated
astronomical problems. To relieve the frustration of a miserable
existence he dreams up in his spare time intricate and daring crimes.
He confides one of his imagined plans to his employer who is full of
admiration for Lecoq's ingenuity but warns: 'When one has your
disposition, and is poor, one will either become a famous thief or a
great detective. Choose.' Whereupon he hands Lecoq a month's pay
in advance and dismisses him. Lecoq takes his employer's words to
heart and with the help of a letter of recommendation from him
obtains a post in the police service. At first the humdrum life of a
novice policeman disappoints him, but his interest is aroused by an
old amateur detective, the ex-pawnbroker Monsieur Tabaret, known
as 'Tirauclair' because of his favourite phrase '*Il faut que cela se tire
au clair*' ('This thing must be cleared up') and greatly respected for
his unusual and ingenious methods of detection. Lecoq becomes his
disciple, encouraged by 'Tirauclair' himself who recognizes in him a
worthy successor.

Lecoq develops his unusual powers of observation and deduction
to the admiration of his peers and superiors (with the exception of
Inspector Gevrol who, already envious of 'Tirauclair', cannot
conceal his jealousy of the old man's protégé). Ambition and a
certain amount of vanity give impetus to Lecoq's work. He becomes
known as *Monsieur* Lecoq and promotion soon follows. Like
'Tirauclair' he believes that appearances are deceptive and he works
on the principle that the true facts of a crime are usually the opposite
from the obvious. His deductions seem miraculous but are
simplicity itself once explained. He carries a comfit box which bears a
portrait on its lid to which he often seems to refer. He lives in the
Rue Montmartre watched over by his old woman servant, Janouille,
an ex-convict found guilty of infanticide and arson but now
staunchly faithful to Lecoq. The door of his lodgings is engraved with

a crowing cock and the inscription 'Toujours Vigilant'. As he becomes more widely known he finds it necessary to develop one of his greatest talents, that of disguise, to escape reprisals from the many criminals he has brought to justice. After years of work in the Sûreté he never appears as himself even before his own men. All his disguises are brilliant, he changes not only his outward appearance but also his character. 'The eye is the thing to be changed – the eye! The art lies in being able to change the eye. That is the secret.' The real Monsieur Lecoq is now only known to old Janouille, although it is quite possible that even Monsieur Lecoq himself can no longer remember how he looks undisguised.

It must surely be true that Monsieur Lecoq is Emile Gaboriau's study from life. Gaboriau was born on 9 November 1832, the son of a notary who determined that Emile should study the law. In defiance of his father's wishes Emile enlisted in the cavalry. After seven years he left the service and became a clerk in Paris. In his spare time he worked as a ghost writer on the criminal romances of feuilletonist Paul Féval and (such is the irony of life) this led him to a closer study of the police court and morgue in search of material. He was studying law after all, although not perhaps in quite the way his father had intended.

In the 1860s Gaboriau began writing on his own account and his first detective story *L'Affaire LeRouge* began as a serial in *Le Pays*, a journal which went bankrupt before the story was completed. Two years later it was published in *Le Soleil* and became an immediate success.

Apart from his study of the law and its enforcement in action he is thought to have been influenced by the memoirs of Vidocq (1775–1857) the infamous French criminal who eventually renounced crime and became the head of the Sûreté. From all these experiences Gaboriau produced the wonderfully clear-headed Lecoq. The first detective to master completely the art of disguise and the first literary ambassador of French criminology. A contribution to world literature which was to influence the detective story for generations to come.

Publications and Performances

Published texts

L'Affaire LeRouge. Originally published in *Le Pays* and *Le Soleil* (Paris), Paris: E. Dentu, 1866.

The Widow LeRouge. Translated from French by Fred Williams and Geo A. O. Ernst, Osgood's Library of Novels no 28, Boston: J. R. Osgood, 1873.

'Gaboriau's Sensational Novels', London: Vizetelly & Co, 1881–4.

The Widow LeRouge. Seaside Library, vol 25, no 515, New York: G. Munro, 1879.

The Widow LeRouge. London: G. Routledge, 1887.

The Widow LeRouge. Secret Service Series no 49, New York: Street & Smith, 1891.

The Widow LeRouge. New York: C. Scribner's Sons, 1900.

The Lerouge Case. New York: Crowell, 1902.

The LeRouge Affair. New York: Caldwell, 1908.

The LeRouge Case. Home Circle Library no 4, London: Federation Press, 1925.

The Widow LeRouge. London: Victor Gollancz, 1929.

The Widow LeRouge. Penguin paperback no 509, Harmondsworth: Penguin, 1945.

Le Dossier 113. Originally serialised in *Le Petit Journal*, 1867, Paris: E. Dentu, 1867.

The Steel Safe, or the Stains and Splendours of New York Life. Adapted by Henry Llewellyn Williams, De Witt's Series of Choice Novels no 10, New York: De Witt, 1868.

File No 113. New York: A. L. Burt, 1875.

File No 113. Seaside Library vol 21, no 408, New York: G. Munro, 1875.

Warrant No 113, or the Mystery of the Steel Safe. Trans H. L. Williams, London: Crown Publishing Co, 1884.

File No 113. 'Caxton' novels, London: G. Routledge, 1887.

New York: P. F. Collier, 1894.

New York: C. Scribner's Sons, 1900.

The Blackmailers – Dossier No 113. Trans Ernest Tristan, Lotus Library, London: Greening, 1907.

File No 113. London: Ward Lock, 1907.

London: Hodder & Stoughton, 1920.

Trans and abridged Marjorie Villiers, London: Harvill, 1953.

Le Crime D'Orcival. Originally serialized in *Le Petit Journal*, 1867, Paris: E. Dentu, 1868.

The Mystery of Orcival. Trans Geo M. Towle, Leisure Hour Series no 4, New York: Holt & Williams, 1871.

Gaboriau's Sensational Novels. London: Vizetelly, 1881–4.

The Mystery of Orcival. New York: J. W. Lovell, 1883.

The Mystery of Orcival. London: G. Routledge, 1887.

The Mystery of Orcival. New York: C. Scribner's Sons, 1900.

Le Crime D'Orcival. Paris: Artheme Fayard, 1924.

The Mystery of Orcival. London: Victor Gollancz, 1929.

The Mystery of Orcival. Penguin paperback no 508, Harmondsworth: Penguin, 1945.

Crime at Orcival. Trans and abridged M. Villiers, London: Harvill Press, 1952.

Monsieur Lecoq. Originally serialized in *Le Petit Journal*, 1869, Paris: E. Dentu, 1869.

Monsieur Lecoq. Trans, Boston: Estes & Lauriat, 1880.

Lecoq the Detective. 'Gaboriau's Sensational Novels', London: Vizetelly, 1881–4.

Monsieur Lecoq. Trans, 2 vols, London: G. Routledge, 1887.

Monsieur Lecoq – The Detective's Dilemma. Trans Sir G. Campbell, London: Ward Lock, 1888.

'The Detective's Dilemma', part I of *Monsieur Lecoq*; 'The Detective's Triumph', part II of *Monsieur Lecoq*; Secret Service Series nos 45, 46, New York: Street & Smith, 1891.

Monsieur Lecoq. London: Hodder & Stoughton, 1917.

Monsieur Lecoq. Abridged, Home Circle Library no 6, London: Federation Press, 1925.

On film

Monsieur Lecoq, Detective (subtitled *The Tragedy at Pepper-box Inn*). Eclair Films, 1914.

File 113. Gaumont Productions, 1932. Lew Cody as Monsieur Lecoq.

In 1967 *Monsieur Lecoq*, a projected film starring Zero Mostel, began filming in the UK and France but was never completed.

There is no record of a theatre production featuring Monsieur Lecoq.

Sergeant Cuff

From **The Moonstone** By **Wilkie Collins**

A fly from the railway drove up as I reached the lodge; and out got
a grizzled, elderly man, so miserably lean that he looked as if he had
not got an ounce of flesh on his bones in any part of him. He was
dressed all in decent black, with a white cravat round his neck. His
face was as sharp as a hatchet, and the skin of it was yellow and dry
and withered as an autumn leaf. His eyes, of a steely light grey, had
a very disconcerting trick, when they encountered your eyes, of
looking as if they expected something more from you than you
were aware of yourself. His walk was soft; his voice was melancholy;
his lanky fingers were hooked like claws. He might have been a
parson, or an undertaker – or anything else you like, except what
he really was. A more complete opposite to Superintendent See-
grave than Sergeant Cuff, and a less comforting officer to look at,
for a family in distress, I defy you to discover, search where you
may.

Wilkie Collins, *The Moonstone*

On immediate acquaintance 'the great Cuff' does not inspire
confidence. It is not so much the slightly sinister air which his soft-
footed almost feline bearing gives him but more the apparent
indifference with which he approaches his cases. Watch him at work,
however, observe his subtle questioning of witnesses, follow, if you
can, the ingenuity of his deductions. He is intuition amazingly
tempered with discretion. He may have been born with his
enveloping air of melancholy or he may have acquired it through his
many years of police service. Professionally chameleon-like, he is all
things to all men.

I sent them in, one by one, as he desired. The cook was the first to
enter the Court of Justice, otherwise my room. She remained but a
short time. Report on coming out: 'Sergeant Cuff is depressed in
his spirits but Sergeant Cuff is a perfect gentleman.' My lady's own
maid followed. Remained much longer. Report on coming out: 'If
Sergeant Cuff doesn't believe a respectable woman, he might keep
his opinion to himself, at any rate!' Penelope went next.
Remained only a moment or two. Report on coming out:
'Sergeant Cuff is much to be pitied. He must have been crossed in
love, father, when he was a young man.' The first housemaid
followed Penelope. Remained, like my lady's maid, a long time.
Report on coming out: 'I didn't enter her ladyship's service, Mr.
Betteredge, to be doubted to my face by a low police officer!'
Rosanna Spearman went next. Remained longer than any of them.
No report on coming out – dead silence, and lips as pale as ashes.
Samuel, the footman, followed Rosanna. Remained a minute or
two. Report on coming out: 'Whoever blacks Sergeant Cuff's
boots ought to be ashamed of himself.' Nancy, the kitchenmaid,
went last. Remained a minute or two. Report on coming out:
'Sergeant Cuff has a heart; *he* doesn't cut jokes, Mr. Betteredge,
with a poor hard-working girl.'

Dedicated as the sergeant is to his work his passion is roses. Planting
them, growing them, watching them, smelling them, arguing over

them, whistling them (in moments of deep thought he is usually heard whistling 'The Last Rose of Summer'). It is his contention, and the subject of many arguments, that the white moss-rose does not require to be budded on to the dog-rose to make it grow well. His ambition is eventual retirement to a quiet spot where he can devote his remaining years to the cultivation of roses.

After twenty years in the police force, during which time he has risen to the top of his profession, dealing largely with the settling of scandals in illustrious families, Sergeant Cuff realizes his ambition and under the motherly eye of a housekeeper he retires to a cottage in Dorking which he immediately surrounds with an almost impenetrable wall of roses. Sadly one of his last cases, the theft from a high-ranking heiress of a precious gem known as the Moonstone, had culminated in his respectful dismissal by the young girl's mother who, while convinced of Cuff's honesty and intelligence, considered him 'fatally misled'. It is not until after this lady's death that he is recalled to the case (by then partially solved) and comes temporarily out of retirement to unravel successfully the final tangled strands of the mystery.

By this time such matters are of secondary importance to him for he has won a more important victory. He has succeeded in growing the white moss-rose without first budding it on the dog-rose.

The plots of *The Notting Hill Mystery* and *The Moonstone*, the first full-length English detective novels, bear certain resemblances. Both deal with crimes committed by remote control, as it were. Both are told entirely through letters and documents and both are *how*dunits. Wilkie Collins's immaculately laid plot manages to combine the search for the perpetrator of the crime with an examination of criminal motivation and methodology – the subtlety of his character-studies make the story believable.

Sergeant Cuff is a detailed study of a talented but world-weary professional on the brink of retirement whose hobby is fast taking over from his work. As with Dickens (who was a close friend of Collins) the professional detective in the story is not merely a question-and-answer machine.

The intricacies of *The Moonstone* could only have been originated and set down by someone absorbed in the twists and turns of the legal procedure. Collins had studied law at Lincoln's Inn and had been called to the bar in 1851. He and Dickens were fascinated by the law and determined to expose both legal and social injustices. While on a trip to Paris with Dickens, Collins bought some old chronicles of French crime. He often used them as a basis for his plots. Collins's favourite among his own works was *The Woman in White*, a tale of mystery and intrigue which the hero sets out to untangle. Opinions differ as to whether or not it is a better book than *The Moonstone*. In accordance with his own wishes, however, the epitaph on his tomb-stone reads:

Author of *The Woman in White*
and other works of fiction.

Publications and Performances

Published texts

'The Moonstone' first appeared in *All the Year Round* in serial form, 4 January–8 August 1868; first appeared in book form in 1868 in three volumes. Publishers: London: Tinsley Bros; New York: Harper & Bros; New York: A. L. Burt.

Select publishers

London: Smith Elder, 1871; New York: Garden City, 1874; New York:
Norman L. Munro, 1884; London: Chatto & Windus, 1895; New York:
The Century Co, 1903; New York: C. Scribner's Sons, 1908, illus John
Sloan; New York: Dodd Mead, 1912; London: T. Nelson, 1925, Nelson's
Classics; London: Harrap's Standard Fiction Library, 1925; World's
Classics, Oxford University Press, 1928, with intro by T. S. Eliot; Collins
Detective Story Club, London: Wm Collins, 1931; London/Glasgow:
Blackie, 1931; Abridged version, London: Queensway Press, 1935; The
Modern Library, 1937, *The Moonstone* and *The Woman in White* in one vol;
Midnite Mysteries, New York Books, 1944; Everyman Library no 979,
London: Dent/Dutton, 1944; World's Classics no 316, intro T. S. Eliot,
New York: H. Milford, 1945; Pyramid Books, Almat Publishing Co, 1950;
London: The Folio Society, 1951, lithographs by Edwin La Dell; Great
Illustrated Classics, New York: Dodd, Mead & Co, 1955; Penguin paperback
no 1072, Harmondsworth: Penguin, 1955; For members of the Limited
Editions Club, New York, illus Dignimont 1959; A Perennial Classic, New
York/Evanston: Harper & Row, 1965; Pan Books no T30, Pan, 1967;
Collins Classics for Today, abridged Joan De Fraine, illus John Sergeant,
London: Wm Collins, 1971.

Play editions

The Moonstone. A dramatic story in three acts, Charles Dickens & Evans,
1877; *The Moonstone*. A mystery play in three acts, London/New York:
Samuel French, 1941.

On film

The Moonstone. Urban Production Company, 1911.

The Moonstone. Pathé Films, 1935. Charles Irwin as Sergeant Cuff.

In the theatre

The Moonstone. The Olympic Theatre, London, 1877. Thomas Swinbourne
as Sergeant Cuff.

Nick Carter

From **The New York Weekly** By **J. R. Coryell**

'Let's search the deck,' said one of them. 'Mebby he didn't go
overboard.'

'Bah! d'ye think he'd stay here? Not much!'

'He's a terror, ain't he?'

'Lightnin's nothin' to that feller.'

'Who is he?'

'Look here, Tony, there's only one man in New York who could
do what he did, an' that's the young devil they call Nick Carter.'

'Ah! the "little giant".'

'That's him.'

F. M. Van Rensselaer Dey, *Nick Carter, Detective*

**Old style Nick Carter. Cover illustration
for** *The Nick Carter Weekly*

After his father has been killed by gangsters, Nick Carter vows to
devote his life to bringing the murderers to justice. He becomes the
pupil of Seth Carter (The Old Detective). Luckily for young Nick he
is blessed with all the qualities essential in one dedicated to the war
against crime – strength, bravery, brain power, a high morality
quotient – and blessed with them in a far higher degree than many of

his calling. His bravery is unassailable, his strength indomitable, his brain power unfathomable and his morality incorruptible. Small wonder then that he is destined to become one of the greats, if not *the* world's greatest detective.

He works with two assistants, Chickering (Chick) Carter and Paddy Garvan. Nick and Chick are not related, but Chick is known as the editor of the chronicled Nick Carter adventures and has shared many of Nick's most hair-raising escapades.

Important among Nick's many accomplishments is his astounding talent for the art of disguise. The possessor of a complete wardrobe and make-up kit in his home, he can effect the most intricate and undetectable change of identity in half an hour. Even more astonishing are his portable outfits. In the space of a few minutes, and given a dark corner or a turned back, he can transform himself from one character into yet another. It is his habit to work as much as possible in disguise, as by remaining incognito his various disguises are 'rendered absolutely impenetrable'.

A chivalrous respecter of the opposite sex, he believes firmly that a man does not fight a woman. In *Scylla, the Sea Robber or Nick Carter and the Queen of Sirens*, a woman, beautiful but evil, penetrated his disguise (for the first and last time in his life). Her triumph was, of course, only temporary but Nick bore this small defeat with fortitude, a gallant compliment and humble acknowledgement of his own lapse:

'"You are almost as neat at turning compliments, Nick Carter, as you are in the matter of disguises," she said.

'"Better, madam; there is no flaw in my remark; there was in my disguise."'

Only one woman has ever captured his heart. This was his wife, Ethel, who sadly met a tragic and untimely death.

Second only to his talent for disguises is his talent for languages, as we learn from *Scylla, the Sea Robber or Nick Carter and the Queen of Sirens*. 'It must be remembered that Nick Carter speaks almost every known language, as well as many that are comparatively unknown.' He can also, of course, lipread all these languages.

Nick has worked all over the world, but particularly in England and his native America. In New York he has an office in Liberty Street which is run by Mr T. Bolt; but it is only the privileged few who know that 'Old Thunderbolt' or 'Joshua Juniper' is a thing of fabrication, an astounding piece of deception, a definitive work in the art of disguise, underneath which are the handsome clean-cut features of Nick Carter, Detective.

Cover design for paperback

Walter Pidgeon (centre) as Nick Carter in
The Phantom Raiders with Florence Rice
and Joseph Schildkraut (MGM, 1940)

Add together the indestructible power and purity of Batman, the
cosmetic artistry of Lecoq, the undeviating manly courage of Rip
Kirby, and you have Nick Carter – a surprisingly early example of a
tough American detective hero. The Nick Carter stories packed the
sort of punch that was ahead of its time. The direct style and instant
unfolding of plot, so well suited to the vernacular of a later style, had
a curious effect when put into nineteenth-century prose. It read rather
like a Victorian melodrama, which, of course, it basically was, as this
extract from *The House of Whispers* will show:

'Great Scott!' Chick exclaimed to himself, 'Mrs. Nell Jordan, instead of the black-eyed daughter. Here to meet Gerry, too, and in
this stealthy fashion. The case is taking a turn I was not looking for.
It may be that the couple are going to elope and bolt for parts
unknown. It won't be the first time that a chauffeur of his stamp has
turned the head of an impressionable lady.'

In spite of the unswerving purity of Nick Carter, who abstained
from every known vice, the writing style is far from inhibited. The
extract below is from *Nick Carter, Detective*.

'I kin stand knifin' a man, or cuttin' a chunk o' cold lead into him,
but when it comes to windin' that cord o' yourn round a feller's
throat, and a-makin' his tongue an' his eye-balls stick out like
fingers, I ain' in it.'

Sex occasionally rears its head in the shape of flashing-eyed villain-
esses whose efforts to thwart Nick can only be described as kinky. In
the long run these she-devils only serve to highlight Nick's unfailing
gallantry towards women, which he enunciates in *Scylla, the Sea
Robber or Nick Carter and the Queen of Sirens*:

25

But even had he been bristling with weapons, he realized that he could not have made use of them to fight his way out.

A man cannot fight a woman; a man will not fight a woman.

He may, on occasion, overpower her and force her to conform to his ideas of right, but he cannot engage in a combat against her as he would do against a man.

The idea of the detective in disguise was first used in Gaboriau's Monsieur Lecoq, but the ability for instant transformation (an example of which appears below in the extracts from *Nick Carter, Detective*) is a Nick Carter original.

When near his destination, he stepped into the hallway for a few moments, and when he emerged, it was in the character of a Negro, whose face was as black as the night which surrounded him . . .

He had not gone twenty feet before his appearance was entirely altered.

From a young man he was changed to a very old one . . .

The entire change had not occupied more than one minute of actual time . . .

The Nick Carter saga was the brain-child of John Coryell and was continued for seventeen years by Frederick Marmaduke Van Rensselaer Dey until mental disturbance led to his tragic suicide. The Carter stories have continued non-stop under the authorship of many writers and a paperback version is still being produced, although the character is unrecognizable as the Nick Carter so stylishly drawn by Coryell and Dey generations ago.

Publications and Performances

Published texts

Nick Carter first appeared in the USA in *The New York Weekly*, 1884, in a serial entitled 'The Old Detective's Pupil'; and subsequently in 'The Nick Carter Library', New York: Street & Smith, and *The Nick Carter Magazine, The New Nick Carter Weekly, The New Magnet Library*.

Carter first appeared in the UK in 'Nick Carter Series', Street & Smith, 1912; *Nick Carter and The Master Rogue (and The Gentleman Plunger, and The Vengeance Trail and other Tales)*, by J. R. Coryell, London: Geo Newnes, 1918–20; *Further Exploits of Nick Carter – Detective*, London: C. A. Pearson, 1920; 'People's Pocket Library'; *Nick Carter's Magazine*.

Under the pseudonym of Nicholas Carter, numerous detective stories were published. Most of them were written by Frederick Van Rensselaer Dey (1865–1922). A few were by John Russell Coryell (1851–1924) who planned the series. Frederick William Davis (1858–1933) also used the pseudonym, but his stories did not have Nick Carter for a hero.

On film

Nick Carter, 1908; *Nick Carter – Bandits in Evening Dress*, 1908; *Nick Carter – Sleeping Pills*, 1909; *Nick Carter in Danger*, 1909. All Itala Films.

Nick Carter as an Acrobat, 1910; *Nick Carter – The Mystery of the White Bed*, 1911; *Nick Carter and the Black-coated Thieves*, 1915. All Eclair Films.

Nick Carter, serial in 15 episodes. International Cine Corporation, 1921. Tom Carrigan as Nick Carter.

Nick Carter – Master Detective, 1939; *Phantom Raiders*, 1940; *Sky Murder*, 1940. All MGM productions. Walter Pidgeon as Nick Carter.

Nick Carter – Va Tout Casser. Florida Films, Paris, 1964. Eddie Constantine as Nick Carter.

Nick Carter et Le Trefle Rouge. Chaumiane-Parc-Films Film Studio Productions, 1965. Eddie Constantine as Nick Carter.

There is no record of any theatre production featuring Nick Carter.

Sherlock Holmes

From **The Sherlock Holmes Stories** By **Sir Arthur Conan Doyle**

His very person and appearance were such as to strike the attention of the most casual observer. In height he was rather over six feet, and so excessively lean that he seemed to be considerably taller. His eyes were sharp and piercing, save during those intervals of torpor to which I have alluded; and his thin, hawk-like nose gave his whole expression an air of alertness and decision. His chin, too, had the prominence and squareness which mark the man of determination. His hands were invariably blotted with ink and stained with chemicals, yet he was possessed of extraordinary delicacy of touch, as I frequently had occasion to observe when I watched him manipulating his fragile philosophical instruments.

The reader may set me down as a hopeless busy-body, when I confess how much this man stimulated my curiosity, and how often I endeavoured to break through the reticence which he showed on all that concerned himself.

Arthur Conan Doyle, *A Study in Scarlet*

His ancestors were country squires. His mother the sister of the French artist Vernet. Holmes is a consultant detective with extraordinary powers of deduction. His work is unnoticed until, while working on chemical experiments at Barts hospital, he is introduced to Dr John Watson MD who becomes his fellow

Basil Rathbone (centre) as Sherlock Holmes in *The Hound of the Baskervilles* (20th Century Fox, 1939)

lodger at No 221B Baker Street, and later his chronicler.

Holmes's knowledge of chemistry and sensational literature is profound and he also has a limited acquaintance with geology and anatomy. He is an expert boxer, swordsman and singlestick player, an excellent actor, a master of disguise, has a practical knowledge of the law and has committed most case-histories to memory. He smokes both cigarettes and a pipe, greatly appreciates classical music and plays a Stradivarius violin. To aid his concentration he will retire with his pipe (a really tricky case is a 'Three Pipe Problem') and his violin. When there is no case to test his prowess, he may sometimes smoke opium and inject cocaine to assuage boredom.

His methods of detection are unique in their simplicity. By observing the everyday details of a person or a situation, usually so trivial they are overlooked by others, he is able to reconstruct an accurate case-history of the crime, working backwards through the effect to the cause.

His clients are varied. From a one-time ship's carpenter (*The Red-headed League*) to a king (*Scandal in Bohemia*). He is often consulted by other detectives when their own powers have failed them, and has frequently solved a case for Inspector Lestrade of Scotland Yard.

Before Dr Watson made the great man world famous, Holmes suffered his bitterest moments reading the newspaper accounts of crimes solved by himself but credited to Lestrade and his colleagues. On 4 May 1891, Holmes was presumed dead when a struggle at the Riechenbach Falls in Switzerland with his arch-enemy Moriarty appeared to topple both men over the edge. Moriarty fell to his death, but Holmes was saved by his knowledge of Japanese wrestling. Realizing that the rest of the Moriarty gang were after his life he fled over the mountains and while the world mourned his death he travelled incognito through Florence, Tibet (where he spent a few days with the Dalai Llama), Persia, Mecca, Khartoum and Montpelier in the south of France, where for some months he researched coal-tar derivatives. His only confidant was his brother Mycroft who financed him and kept his rooms at Baker Street untouched. After three years, hearing that only one of his enemies remained at large, and enticed by a particular mystery baffling Scotland Yard, he reappears in London and startles the world – in particular his landlady, Mrs Hudson, and his old friend, Dr Watson.

His brother Mycroft, seven years his senior, is gifted with the same powers of observation and deduction as Sherlock but lack of practicality, ambition and energy prevent him from earning his livelihood as a detective. Sherlock considers Mycroft's mind to be keener than his own and has often successfully consulted his brother when confronted by a problem which even his astute brain cannot fathom.

There has been only one woman in Sherlock Holmes's life. The late Irene Adler, born in New Jersey in 1858, ex-opera singer, Prima Donna of the Imperial Opera of Warsaw, once outwitted Sherlock Holmes (*A Scandal in Bohemia*). Cold, precise and analytical he had always been indifferent to women, but Irene Adler challenged him on his own ground and won the contest. For him she surpasses all her sex. He refers to her always as '*the* woman' and there can never be another.

The launching of Sherlock Holmes was a quiet affair. Arthur Conan Doyle was an unsuccessful doctor who wrote a little to supplement his income. His first crop of short stories and one full-length novel were at first unremunerative, but the turning-point came in 1886. He had always been fascinated by the detective stories of Poe and Gaboriau (the influence of Dupin and Lecoq are plain in the Sherlock

John Neville as Sherlock Holmes (on location) in *A Study in Terror* (Compton-Cameo Films, 1965)

Holmes stories), and he began to develop a character based on Dr Joseph Bell, the eminent surgeon who had been his tutor at Edinburgh University. In his *Memories and Adventures* (1924) Doyle wrote:

> Gaboriau had rather attracted me by the neat dove-tailing of his plots, and Poe's masterful detective, M. Dupin, had from boyhood been one of my heroes. But could I bring an addition of my own? I thought of my old teacher, Joe Bell, of his eagle face, of his curious ways, of his eerie trick of spotting details. If he were a detective he would surely reduce this fascinating but unorganized business to something nearer to an exact science. I would try if I could get this effect.

The first Holmes story, *A Study in Scarlet*, proved difficult to sell but eventually Ward Lock bought the manuscript for £25 and Sherlock Holmes made his first appearance in the twenty-eighth edition of *Beeton's Christmas Annual*, 1887. But it wasn't until 1890, when the second Holmes adventure (*The Sign of Four*) was published in the American *Lippincott's Magazine*, that success seemed likely and Doyle was able to give up his medical practice. In July 1891 *The Strand Magazine* began to publish the stories and Sherlock Holmes built up a popularity which grew into a cult that has outlived its author.

Doyle looked on Holmes purely as a money spinner. He wanted to be known for his other literary work, but Holmes was beginning to take over his life and reputation. In 1893 he killed off Holmes. (Doyle wrote of the 'death' of Holmes as occurring in 1891.) But by this time it was not just a fictional detective who met his death over the Reichenbach Falls, but a national hero. The public outcry was unprecedented and Doyle was given no peace until, in 1903, and now Sir Arthur Conan Doyle, he resurrected The Great Man.

Doyle died on 7 July 1930 and no amount of public outcry could resurrect him. Sherlock Holmes, however, has become a legend and his shrine can be found at his old residence, 221B Baker Street, where his rooms are arranged just as they would have been in his lifetime; and an employee of the building society which owns the building is engaged to answer the hundreds of letters which pour in addressed to Holmes. Sherlock Holmes societies exist in all parts of the world and it is difficult to think of a fictional character so loved and so firmly believed in by so many people.

Publications and Performances

Published texts

A Study in Scarlet. London: Ward Lock, 1888; New York: A. L. Burt, 1888. Originally published in *Beeton's Christmas Annual*, 1887.

Sign of Four. London: Spencer Blackett, 1890; New York: Hurst, 1890. Originally published in *Lippincott's Magazine*, February 1890.

Adventures of Sherlock Holmes. London: Geo Newnes, 1892; New York: Harper, 1892. Originally published in *The Strand Magazine*, London, 1891–2.

Memoirs of Sherlock Holmes. London: Geo Newnes, 1894; New York: Harper, 1894. The first American edition included 'The Cardboard Box', omitted from the London edition at the author's request.

Hound of the Baskervilles. London: Geo Newnes, 1902; New York: McClure Phillips, 1902. Originally published in *The Strand Magazine*, London, 1901.

Return of Sherlock Holmes. London: Geo Newnes, 1905; New York: McClure Phillips, 1906. Originally published in *The Strand Magazine*, 1903–4 and *Collier's Magazine*, New York, 1903–5.

The Valley of Fear. London: John Murray, 1915; New York: Geo H. Doran, 1915. Originally published in *The Strand Magazine*, 1914–15.

His Last Bow. London: John Murray, 1917; New York: Geo H. Doran, 1917. Originally published in *The Strand Magazine*, 1917.

Case Book of Sherlock Holmes. London: John Murray, 1927; New York: Geo H. Doran, 1927.

On film (Silents)

Sherlock Holmes Baffled. American Multigraph & Biograph Co, 1900.

Adventures of Sherlock Holmes. Vitagraph (USA), 1903. Title in UK *Held to Ransom*. Maurice Costello as Holmes.

Rival Sherlock Holmes. Ambrosio (Italy), 1907.

Sherlock Holmes in the Great Murder Mystery. Crescent Film Manufacturing Co, 1908.

Sherlock Holmes. Nordisk Film Co (Copenhagen), 1908. Forrest Holger Madsen as Holmes.

The Latest Triumph of Sherlock Holmes. Gaumont (France), 1909.

The Speckled Band, The Reigate Squire, Beryl Coronet, Adventure of the Copper Beeches, Mystery of Boscombe Vale, The Stolen Papers, Silver Blaze, The Musgrave Ritual. Eclair Films, 1912. Georges Treville as Holmes.

The Sign of Four. Thanhouser (USA), 1913. Harry Benham as Holmes.

Der Hund von Baskerville. Vitascope (Germany), 1914. Alwin Neuss as Holmes.

A Study in Scarlet. Samuelson Film Manufacturing, 1914. James Bragington as Holmes.

A Study in Scarlet. Universal, 1914. Francis Ford as Holmes.

Sherlock Holmes. Essanay, 1916. William Gillette as Holmes.

The Valley of Fear. Samuelson Film Manufacturing, 1916. H. A. Saintsbury as Holmes.

Der Hund von Baskerville. Vitascope (Germany), 1917.

In 1921 Stoll Picture Productions made a series of films, of which 16 are recorded, under the general title *The Adventures of Sherlock Holmes*. In 1922 a second series followed, entitled *The Further Adventures of Sherlock Holmes*, and in 1923 *The Last Adventures of Sherlock Holmes*. In all of these Holmes was played by Eille Norwood.

Sherlock Holmes (title in the UK *Moriarty*). Goldwyn Corporation, 1922. John Barrymore as Holmes. At the end of this film Holmes marries Miss Alice Faulkner, played by Carol Dempster.

Clive Brook (in disguise) in the first Sherlock Holmes 'talkie' *The Return of Sherlock Holmes* **(Paramount, 1929)**

Der Hund von Baskerville. Sudfilm, 1929. Carlyle Blackwell as Holmes.

Sound

Return of Sherlock Holmes, Paramount, 1929. Clive Brook as Holmes.

A 15-minute talking short featuring Conan Doyle telling how he originated the Holmes character, and sending greetings to his admirers. Fox/Movietone, 1929.

The Sleeping Cardinal, First Division, 1930; *The Sign of the Four*, World Wide, 1932; *The Missing Rembrandt*, Paramount, 1932; *The Triumph of Sherlock Holmes*, Twickenham Films, 1935. Arthur Wontner as Holmes.

The Speckled Band. First Division, 1931. Raymond Massey as Holmes.

Hound of the Baskervilles. First Division, 1932. Robert Rendel as Holmes.

Sherlock Holmes. Fox, 1932. Clive Brook as Holmes. Based on *The Red-headed League*.

A Study in Scarlet. Fox, 1933. Reginald Owen as Holmes. Reginald Owen had played Dr Watson in a 1932 Sherlock Holmes film, and possessed the distinction of being the only actor to have played both parts.

The Silver Blaze (title in USA *Murder at the Baskervilles*). Twickenham Film Productions, 1937. Arthur Wontner as Holmes.

Hound of the Baskervilles. 20th Century Fox, 1939; *Adventures of Sherlock Holmes*, 20th Century Fox, 1939. Basil Rathbone as Holmes.

With Nigel Bruce co-starring as Dr Watson, Basil Rathbone went on to make 12 films for Universal Pictures between 1942 and 1946:
Sherlock Holmes in Washington, 1942; *Sherlock Holmes and the Secret Weapon*, 1942; *Sherlock Holmes and the Voice of Terror*, 1943; *Sherlock Holmes Faces Death*, 1943; *Spider Woman*, 1944; *Pearl of Death*, 1944; *The Scarlet Claw*, 1944; *The House of Fear*, 1945; *The Woman in Green*, 1945; *Pursuit to Algiers*, 1945; *Terror by Night*, 1946; *Dressed to Kill* (title in UK *Sherlock Holmes and the Secret Code*).

Adventure of the Speckled Band. Marshall Grant Realm-Tele Productions, 1949. Alan Napier as Holmes.

Hound of the Baskervilles. Hammer Films, 1959. Peter Cushing as Holmes.

A Study in Terror. Compton/Cameo (UK), 1965. John Neville as Holmes.

The Private Life of Sherlock Holmes. Mirisch, 1970. Robert Stephens as Holmes.

In the theatre

Under the Clock (1893). Extravaganza in one act by C. H. E. Brookfield and Seymour Hicks. Royal Court Theatre, London, 1893. Music by Edward Jones. C. H. E. Brookfield as Sherlock Holmes.

Sherlock Holmes by Charles Rogers. Theatre Royal, Glasgow, 1894. John Webb as Sherlock Holmes.

Sherlock Holmes by Arthur Conan Doyle and William Gillette. Garrick Theatre, New York, November 1899. William Gillette as Sherlock Holmes. (Originally produced at the Star Theatre, Buffalo, October 1899.)

The Bank of England by Max Goldberg. Shakespeare Theatre, Clapham Junction, London, 1900. John F. Preston as Sherlock Holmes.

Sherlock Holmes by Arthur Conan Doyle and William Gillette. Lyceum Theatre, London, September 1901. William Gillette as Sherlock Holmes. (First produced in Great Britain at the Shakespeare Theatre, Liverpool, September 1901.)

Sherlock Holmes, Detective or The Sign of the Four. Melodrama in four acts by John Arthur Fraser. Hopkins Theatre, Chicago, 1901. Richard Butler as Sherlock Holmes.

Sign of the Four by Charles P. Rice. West End Theatre, New York, 1903. Walter Edwards as Sherlock Holmes.

The Painful Predicament of Sherlock Holmes. One-act curtain raiser by William Gillette. William Gillette as Sherlock Holmes; Charles Chaplin as Billy.

Sherlock Holmes by Ferdinand Bonn. Berliner Theatre, Berlin, 1906. Ferdinand Bonn as Sherlock Holmes.

Der Hund von Baskerville by Ferdinand Bonn. Berliner Theatre, Berlin, 1907. Ferdinand Bonn as Sherlock Holmes.

Sherlock Holmes by Pierre De Courcelle. Theatre Antoine, Paris, 1907. Firmin Gemier as Sherlock Holmes.

The Speckled Band by Arthur Conan Doyle. Adelphi Theatre, London, 1910. H. A. Saintsbury as Sherlock Holmes.

Raffle–ing of Sherlock Holmes. One-act curtain raiser by N. Thorpe Mayne. Grand Theatre, Fulham, 1913.

The Crown Diamond. One-act play by Arthur Conan Doyle. London Coliseum, 1921. Dennis Neilson Terry as Sherlock Holmes.

The Return of Sherlock Holmes by J. E. Harold Terry and Arthur Rose. Princes Theatre, London, 1923. Eille Norwood as Sherlock Holmes.

The Holmeses of Baker Street by Basil Mitchell. Lyric Theatre, London, 1933. Felix Aylmer as Sherlock Holmes.

The Great Detective (a ballet). Choreography by Margaret Dale, music by Richard Arnell. Sadlers Wells, London, 1953. Kenneth Macmillan as the Great Detective.

Sherlock Holmes by Ouida Rathbone. Majestic Theatre, Boston, Mass, 1953, and later at the Century Theatre, New York, 1953. Basil Rathbone as Sherlock Holmes.

Baker Street (a musical). Book by Jerome Coppersmith, music and lyrics by Marian Grudeff and Raymond Jessell. Broadway Theatre, New York, 1965. Fritz Weaver as Sherlock Holmes.

Sherlock Holmes and the Speckled Band by David Buxton. Colchester Repertory Theatre, 1968. Roger Heathcott as Sherlock Holmes.

Sherlock Holmes (revival) by Arthur Conan Doyle and William Gillette. Royal Shakespeare Company at the Aldwych Theatre, London, 1974. John Wood as Sherlock Holmes.

Sherlock's Last Case by Matthew Lang. Open Space Theatre, London, 1974. Julian Glover as Sherlock Holmes.

Sherlock Holmes of Baker Street by John Southworth. Ipswich Drama Centre, 1974. Richard Franklin as Sherlock Holmes.

Television

In UK: BBC Television series. Alan Wheatley as Sherlock Holmes, 1951; Douglas Wilmer as Sherlock Holmes, 1965; Peter Cushing as Sherlock Holmes, 1968.

In USA: *Adventures of Sherlock Holmes*. Sheldon Reynolds Productions, 1954. Ronald Howard as Sherlock Holmes.

Inspector Bucket

From **Bleak House** By **Charles Dickens**

Mr. Snagsby is dismayed to see, standing with an attentive face between himself and the lawyer, at a little distance from the table, a person with a hat and stick in his hand, who was not there when he himself came in, and has not since entered by the door or by either of the windows. There is a press in the room, but its hinges have not creaked, nor has a step been audible upon the floor. Yet this third person stands there, with his attentive face, and his hat and stick in his hands, and his hands behind him, a composed and quiet listener. He is a stoutly built, steady-looking, sharp-eyed man in black, of about middle-age. Except that he looks at Mr. Snagsby as if he were going to take his portrait, there is nothing remarkable about him at first sight but his ghostly manner of appearing.

'Don't mind this gentleman,' says Mr. Tulkinghorn, in his quiet way. 'This is only Mr. Bucket.'

Charles Dickens, *Bleak House*

'Inspector Bucket of the Detective' is a professional and as with all professionals (of whatever profession) his hardest work is done without anyone being in the least bit aware that he has been doing it at all. He is a methodical man, dedicated to his art. A self-taught observer of anything within reach of observation, 'in case he should ever find such knowledge useful'. A stout middle-aged man he is the possessor of a podgy forefinger of which he makes full use.

'Friendly behaviour of Mr Bucket'. Original illustration for *Bleak House* by Phiz (H. K. Browne), 1852

He puts it to his ears, and it whispers information; he puts it to his lips, and it enjoins him to secrecy; he rubs it over his nose, and it sharpens his scent; he shakes it before a guilty man, and it charms him to destruction.

The Augurs of the Detective Temple invariably predict, that when Mr. Bucket and that finger are in much conference, a terrible avenger will be heard of before long.

Mrs Bucket shares her husband's enthusiasm for his work and he is proud of her undoubted talents as his unofficial assistant. The only shadow over their otherwise happy marriage is their childlessness.

Bucket is often seen strolling the dirty back alleys of London, visiting the houses and their inhabitants. He can be kindly, generous and friendly, but benign as he sometimes is these feelings do not stand in the way of duty. Rogues and villains abound in London, it is his job to know them and he is compassionate but unsentimental.

His brother and his brother-in-law, he has said, are in service. His father rose from a page through footman and butler to steward and then became an inn-keeper. Inspector Bucket has experience of persons in all stratas of society. He is respectfully firm with the aristocracy, who in no way intimidate him.

The chancery case, Jarndyce and Jarndyce, disputing the distribution of the Jarndyce estate and protracted over many years, has entangled many people in its side-issues, including the aristocratic Dedlock family (when speaking to Sir Leicester Dedlock Inspector Bucket always addresses him as 'Sir Leicester Dedlock, Baronet'). The case involves the murder of the lawyer, Mr Tulkinghorn. Bucket runs to earth the murderess, Lady Dedlock's French maid, and instigates a desperate but unsuccessful attempt to prevent the suicide of the tragic Lady Dedlock. He also produces evidence which brings hope of a satisfactory end to the case of Jarndyce and Jarndyce. Unfortunately it is too late for the case is concluded suddenly by the discovery that the estate itself has been slowly devoured by costs incurred during its lengthy time in Chancery.

Inspector Bucket has a talent for appearing quietly and suddenly at unexpected times and in unexpected places. He often seems to follow his clues in the wrong direction and it is not until a case is safely solved that his direction is seen to have been unerringly right. He is considered by some to be a 'close' man while others are surprised to find themselves confiding in him in the same way that he appears to confide in them. All agree that Inspector Bucket is deep. Very deep.

Dickens was no stranger to the law. He encountered it in his boyhood when his father was imprisoned for debt. Further, his first job, after completing a broken education, was as office boy to a Symonds Inn solicitor, Charles Molloy; and his second job was office boy to lawyers Ellis and Blackmore's of Gray's Inn, graduating to shorthand writer at Doctors Commons. In later life Dickens's close friends included John Forster, a barrister and literary critic who became Dickens's most important biographer, and Wilkie Collins, barrister and author of *The Moonstone*, one of the earliest Whodunits in literature.

When *Bleak House* was written Peel's Metropolitan Police Act had been in force for little more than twenty years and an official detective must still have been something of a novelty. (Bucket carefully introduces himself as 'Inspector Bucket of the Detective'.) Bucket would certainly have been the result of Dickens's observations while working in the law courts, and so his character has range and depth and is more than the mere representative of an official body.

Bleak House was first published in nineteen monthly parts during 1852 and 1853, and in book form in 1853.

Publications and Performances

First publications of Bleak House

Bleak House was first published March 1852–September 1853, 20 episodes in 19 parts, illus 'Phiz', London: Bradbury & Evans; first published in book form in 1853, illus 'Phiz', London: Bradbury & Evans; New York: Harper & Bros.

Published texts

With frontispiece by H. K. Browne ('Phiz'), 'Cheap edition of the works of Mr. Charles Dickens', London: Bradbury & Evans, 1858.

Part of the 'New Two Shilling Series', London: W. Nicholson, 1890.

With an introduction by G. K. Chesterton, Everyman's Library no 236, London: J. M. Dent, 1907; New York: E. P. Dutton, 1907.

Collins Illustrated Classics no 47, illus W. H. C. Groome, London: Collins Clear Type Press, 1908.

New York: University Society, 1908.

Universal edition, London: Chapman & Hall, 1914; New York: C. Scribner's Sons, 1914.

Nelson's Classics, London: T. Nelson, 1925.

Limited edition, facsimile of wrapper and title pages of first edn, London: Macmillan, 1933.

Nonesuch Press, London: Bloomsbury, 1938.

Illus Robert Ball, New York: Heritage Press, 1942.

Intro Sir Osbert Sitwell, London/New York: Oxford University Press, 1948.

Illus 'Phiz', Odhams Press, 1950.

New York: Dodd Mead, 1951.

Intro R. Brimley Johnson, London: Wm Collins, 1953.

Arranged for modern reading, New York: Literary Guild of America, 1953.

Illus 'Phiz', Macdonald's Illustrated Classics, no 32. London: Macdonald, 1955.

Illus Edward Ardizonne, abridged Percy S. Winter, Oxford University Press (Sheldon Library), 1955.

Intro Morton Dauwen Zabel, Boston: Houghton Mifflin, 1956.

Afterword Geoffrey Tillotson, New American Library (Signet Classics), 1964.

Ed Norman Page, 27 original illus by Hablot K. Browne ('Phiz'), Penguin English Library, Harmondsworth: Penguin, 1971.

On film

Bleak House. Ideal Films, 1920. Clifford Heatherley as Bucket.

Bleak House. (Tense Moments from Great Plays), BEF Masters Productions (UK), 1922. Harry J. Worth as Bucket.

In 1962 Agatha Christie was contracted by MGM to write a screenplay for *Bleak House* but the project was never realized.

In the theatre

Jo by J. P. Burnett. Prince of Wales, Liverpool, 1875. J. P. Burnett as Bucket; revived at the Globe Theatre, London, 1876 and at the Strand Theatre, London, 1885.

Bleak House, or Poor Jo by George Lander. Pavilion Theatre, London, 1876. F. Thomas as Bucket.

Poor Jo by Terry Hurst. Surrey Theatre, 1876.

Jo the Waif by Herbert Rhoyds. Theatre Royal, Greenwich, 1876.

Bleak House, or Poor Jo by Eliza Thorne. Alexandra Opera House, Sheffield, 1876.

Poor Little Jo by Murray Wood. Park Theatre, New York, 1877.

Poor Jo by H. Davenport. Theatre Royal, Southampton, 1878.

Jo the Waif, or the Mystery of Chesney Wold (author unknown). Rotunda Theatre, Liverpool, 1881.

Move On, or The Crossing Sweeper by James Mortimer. Grand Theatre, Islington, 1883. R. C. Lyons as Bucket.

Lady Dedlock's Secret by J. Palgrave Simpson. Opera Comique, 1884. Howard Russell as Bucket.

Move On, or Jo the Outcast by James Mortimer. Lyric Theatre, London, 1892. Henry Bedford as Bucket.

Jo by J. P. Burnett (revival). Drury Lane, London, 1896. Frank MacVicars as Bucket.

Bleak House, or Events in the Life of Jo by Oswald Brand. The Grand, Islington, London, 1902. W. R. Sutherland as Bucket.

Bleak House by J. Stilwell and W. Benson. Theatre Royal, Margate, 1903.

Lady Dedlock by P. Kester. Ambassadors Theater, New York, 1928.

Bleak House. Three-act version for public reading by Emlyn Williams. Cardiff, and Edinburgh Festival, 1952.

Television

Bleak House. BBC Television, 1959. Richard Pearson as Bucket.

Dramatizations of Bleak House

Bleak House, or Poor Jo. In four acts, adapted by George Lander, Dick's Standard Plays, no 388, 1883.

Lady Dedlock's Secret. In four acts, based on an episode in the novel, adapted by B. J. Palgrave Simpson, French's acting edition, no 1822, London: Samuel French, 1885.

Father Brown

From **The Father Brown Series** By **G. K. Chesterton**

> The little priest was so much the essence of those Eastern flats; he had a face as round and dull as a Norfolk dumpling; he had eyes as empty as the North Sea; he had several brown paper parcels, which he was quite incapable of collecting. The Eucharistic Congress had doubtless sucked out of their local stagnation many such creatures, blind and helpless, like moles disinterred. Valentin was a sceptic in the severe style of France, and could have no love for priests. But he could have pity for them, and this one could have provoked pity in anybody. He had a large, shabby umbrella, which constantly fell on the floor. He did not seem to know which was the right end of his return ticket.

> G. K. Chesterton, *The Innocence of Father Brown*
> ('The Blue Cross')

> Know then thyself, presume not God to scan;
> The proper study of mankind is man.
> Alexander Pope, 'An Essay on Man'

A dumpy Roman Catholic priest, moon-faced, short-sighted and mild to the point of blandness is an unlikely detective. But Father Brown, with almost incongruous simplicity, can unravel a mystery hopelessly baffling to a less straightforward mind.

Formerly priest for the village of Cobhole in Essex, the church has spread the roots of Father Brown to many different parts of the world from Hartlepool (where he was a curate) to Scotland, London, Cornwall, Spain, France, Ireland and the northern coast of South America (where he officiated as 'something between a missionary and a parish priest'). He regards his exploits in detection as an extension of his work as a priest. His interest is particularly in the criminal rather than the crime. Divine intervention is not in his line, as he states in 'The Miracle of Moon Crescent': 'I believe in miracles. I believe in man-eating tigers, but I don't see them running about everywhere.' The label 'Saintly Sleuth', once suggested by an American admirer, makes him shudder, for this enigmatic little man with his deceptively insignificant looks and unassuming manner has a firm hold on the realities of life, a faith as enduring as the pyramids, a sad but down-to-earth acceptance of his own and others' frailties and an unexpectedly thorough knowledge of the underworld gleaned from the confessional, as Father Brown says in 'The Blue Cross': '"One gets to know, you know," he added, rubbing his head again with the same sort of desperate apology. "We can't help being priests. People come and tell us these things."'

The works of Father Brown were first brought to the public notice when, after several encounters with him, Flambeau, the famous French criminal, a giant both in physique and notoriety, gave up his life of crime and became a private detective in England. A firm and lasting friendship grew up between the two men. Flambeau, after falling in love with and marrying a Spanish lady, now lives in a castle in Spain where he is content to tend the estate and bring up his large family. As he explains in 'The Secret of Flambeau'.

> I stole for twenty years with these two hands; I fled from the police on these two feet. . . . Have I not heard the sermons of the

Alec Guinness as Father Brown in *Father Brown* (Columbia, 1954)

righteous and seen the cold stare of the respectable. . . . Only my friend told me that he knew exactly why I stole; and I have never stolen since.

The enduring Father Brown stumps around quietly resolving the complexities of crime with his common-sense approach. When asked about his methods of crime-solving he admits that they involve rather more the absence of method ('absence of mind too, I'm afraid'). The secret which he eventually unfolds in 'The Secret of Father Brown' is his ability to empathize with others and not to observe objectively as a scientist:

I mean that I really did see myself, and my real self, committing the murders. I didn't actually kill the men by material means; but that's not the point. Any brick or bit of machinery might have killed them by material means. I mean that I thought and thought about how a man might come to be like that, until I realized that I really *was* like that, in everything except actual final consent to the action.

Perhaps for Father Brown, involved as he is with the baring of souls, this solution comes naturally.

The English have always tended to excel as amateurs, and in the world of fictional crime some of the most entertaining sleuths have indeed been English amateurs. Miss Marple, Simon Templar, Philip Trent. But surely the most original of them all is Father Brown. The work of a Roman Catholic priest would seem to be far from conducive to the business of trailing criminals. Chesterton himself admitted (in his autobiography) that the chances of a Catholic priest having time to spare for the pursuit of criminals, and the coincidence of his being at the scene of so many murders, are all somewhat unlikely:

There is also in the conception, as in nearly everything I have ever written, a good deal of inconsistency and inaccuracy on minor points; not the least of such flaws being the general suggestion that Father Brown had nothing in particular to do, except hang about in any household where there was likely to be a murder.

He was at great pains to refute the widely held view that a priest can know little of the sordidness of vice and crime in the secular world. The point is particularly emphasized in an early Father Brown story 'The Blue Cross' and in Chesterton's autobiography.

37

The priest alluded to was Father John O'Connor of Bradford on whom Chesterton was to base Father Brown. Only partly, however. Father Brown was shabby, shapeless and clumsy while Father O'Connor was neat, delicate and dexterous. But these were only the externals and it was the 'inner intellectual qualities' of Father O'Connor that inspired Chesterton.

Gilbert Keith Chesterton was born at Campden Hill, London, on 29 May 1874. He was educated at St Paul's School (where he became the close friend of Hilaire Belloc and E. C. Bentley, author of the Trent novels) and afterwards at the Slade School of Art. He was known as an essayist, novelist and poet. In 1901 he married Frances Blogg and in 1922 he became a Roman Catholic. He died on 14 June 1936 at his home in Beaconsfield.

Publications and Performances

Published texts

The Innocence of Father Brown. Eight full page plates by Sydney Seymour Lucas, illus Will Foster, London: Cassell, 1911; New York: John Lane, 1911.

The Wisdom of Father Brown. London: Cassell, 1914; New York: Macaulay 1914.

The Incredulity of Father Brown. London: Cassell, 1926; New York: Dodd, Mead, 1926.

The Secret of Father Brown. London: Cassell, 1927; New York: A. L. Burt, 1927.

The Father Brown Stories. Omnibus edition containing 'The Innocence, Wisdom, Incredulity and Secret of Father Brown'. London: Cassell, 1929.

The Father Brown Omnibus. New York: Dodd, Mead, 1933.

The Scandal of Father Brown. London: Cassell, 1935; New York: Dodd, Mead, 1935.

La Naiveco de Pastro Brown. Esperantigis D – ro Cecil Bean, Esperanto Publishing, 1937.

The Pocket Book of Father Brown. New York: Pocket Books, 1943.

The Innocence of Father Brown. Penguin paperback no 765, Harmondsworth: Penguin, 1950.

Father Brown (selected stories). Intro Ronald Knox, World's Classics no 547, Oxford University Press, 1955.

The Incredulity of Father Brown, Penguin paperback no 1069, Harmondsworth: Penguin, 1958.

Father Brown Stories. Illus Edward Ardizonne, London: Folio Society, 1959.

The Father Brown Book. London: Cassell, 1959.

The Second Father Brown Book. London: Cassell, 1959.

The Father Brown Book. Ed for younger readers by Andrew Scotland, Ulverscroft Large Print Series, Ulverscroft: F. A. Thorpe, 1965.

On film

Father Brown, Detective. Paramount, 1935. Walter Connolly as Father Brown.

Father Brown (title in USA *The Detective*). Columbia, 1954. Alec Guinness as Father Brown.

Television

Father Brown (series). ATV Productions, 1974. Kenneth More as Father Brown.

There is no record of any theatre production featuring Father Brown.

Philip Trent

**From Trent's Last Case; Trent Intervenes; Trent's Own Case
By Edmund Clerihew Bentley (later with Warner Allen)**

Mr. Cupples uttered an exclamation of pleasure as a long, loosely-built man, much younger than himself, stepped from the car and mounted the verandah, flinging his hat on a chair. His high-boned, quixotic face wore a pleasant smile; his rough tweed clothes, his hair and short moustache were tolerably untidy.

'Cupples, by all that's miraculous!' cried the man, pouncing on Cupples before he could rise, and seizing his outstretched hand in a hard grip. 'My luck is serving me today,' the newcomer went on spasmodically. 'This is the second slice within an hour. How are you, my best of friends? And why are you here? Why sit'st thou by that ruined breakfast? Dost thou its former pride recall, or ponder how it passed away? I *am* glad to see you!'

E. C. Bentley, *Trent's Last Case*

Above all Philip Trent is concerned with art. The son of an artist he achieved recognition with his paintings while still in his twenties. His work sells, helped by his open almost boyish charm, also, no doubt, by his father's reputation. His upbringing and an Oxford education has given him a sound classical grounding. Besides art and its history he loves music and poetry and is liable to sprinkle an otherwise normal conversation with quotations from English, Greek, French, German or any other literature, a form of one-upmanship which in him is not as irritating as it should be. He is an experienced traveller, being especially fond of France, a keen golfer, swimmer and pipe smoker. He enjoys good food and wine (has probably not had much experience of any other) and, slightly bizarre, is a connoisseur of shoes. His natural exuberance is luckily tempered with a sensitive regard for other people. Perhaps it is the finely tuned eye of the artist that helps his unexpectedly penetrating assessment of character. He has a dislike of undistributed wealth, a touch of the irreverence of socialism so often found in those born into financial security.

Detection entered his life by mistake while he was reading a newspaper account of a much-discussed murder committed in a train. He began to pick on clues which, although neglected by Scotland Yard, seemed obvious to him. On the same day, working only from newspaper reports, he sent a letter to the editor of the *Record*, drawing attention to the significance of evidence hitherto overlooked. The editor, Sir James Molloy, printed the letter in bold type, a new suspect was arrested and made a full confession.

Sir James established a friendship with Trent, offering him another assignment with the newspaper. The success of this was followed at intervals by several others and Philip Trent soon found himself more famous as detective than artist. He never abandoned his true profession, however, keeping his sleuthing as a sideline. His friendship and collaboration with the detectives of Scotland Yard proved mutually helpful. Trent is not infallible and is very liable to put two and two together and come up with five.

After his marriage to Mabel Manderson, the widow of a murdered millionaire, he bought an old manor house in the Cotswolds and divides his time between the country and his studio flat in St John's Wood. Now a family man his detective work is very rare and he continually protests his retirement from sleuthing – although the occasional good case is hard to resist.

One of the most interesting facets of Edmund Clerihew Bentley's Philip Trent is his fallibility. Until his coming the sleuths had been unbeatable – with the exception perhaps of Sergeant Cuff, but this was due more to his clients' lack of co-operation than his own shortcomings. Through their individual methods Dupin, Lecoq, Nick Carter, Holmes, Father Brown and Inspector Bucket were unfailingly right in the end. Trent is a wizard at finding the right clues and following them through in the right direction, but just occasionally he comes unstuck in the final analysis. It doesn't matter terribly of course because there's always someone to provide a piece of evidence that points to the correct solution or, as in *Trent's Last Case*, the final solution is related to him by the number-one witness.

Edmund Clerihew Bentley was well known for his humorous writing. While at school (St Paul's) he invented a form of biographical nonsense rhymes which became known as 'Clerihews':

> Sir Humphrey Davy
> Abominated gravy
> He lived in the odium
> Of having discovered sodium.

It is not surprising that in some parts of the Trent books Mr Bentley's tongue is very definitely in his cheek. In *Trent's Own Case* he introduces a Mr Clerihew, a wine merchant who is a connoisseur of every aspect of his own wares (including the history of corks) and who rather enjoys the sound of his own voice.

Bentley published three volumes of his own nonsense verses. They were illustrated by G. K. Chesterton (author of the Father Brown books), who had been his close friend since their school days at St Paul's and to whom *Trent's Last Case* is dedicated. The two men were great admirers of each other's work. Bentley stated that the main influence in his life had been his association with Chesterton. Chesterton called *Trent's Last Case* 'The finest detective story of modern times.'

Publications and Performances

Published texts

Trent's Last Case (title in USA *The Woman in Black*). London: T. Nelson, 1913; New York: Grosset & Dunlap, 1913.

Trent's Last Case. New York: A. A. Knopf, 1929.

Trent's Last Case. (Fifty modern English writers presented by W. Somerset Maugham.) New York: Doubleday, Doran, 1933.

Trent's Last Case. London: T. Nelson, 1936.

Trent's Own Case. In conjunction with H. W. Allen. London: Constable, 1936; New York: Grosset & Dunlap, 1936; New York: A. A. Knopf, 1936.

Trent's Last Case. Penguin paperback no 78, Harmondsworth: Penguin, 1937.

Trent Intervenes. London: T. Nelson, 1938; New York: Grosset & Dunlap, 1938; New York: A. A. Knopf, 1938.

Trent's Own Case. Penguin paperback no 543, Harmondsworth: Penguin, 1942.

Trent Intervenes. Penguin paperback no 915, Harmondsworth: Penguin, 1953.

Trent's Case Book. Comprising *Trent's Last Case*, *Trent's Own Case*, and *Trent Intervenes*, New York: A. A. Knopf, 1953.

Trent's Last Case. Pan Books, 1965.

Trent's Last Case. Retold by E. L. Black, Streamline Books, London: T. Nelson, 1966.

On film

Trent's Last Case. Walturdaw Productions, 1920. Gregory Scott as Trent.

Trent's Last Case. Fox, 1929. Raymond Griffiths as Trent.

Trent's Last Case. British Lion, 1952. Michael Wilding as Trent.

There is no record of any theatre production featuring Philip Trent.

Michael Wilding as Philip Trent with Margaret Lockwood and Orson Welles in *Trent's Last Case* (British Lion, 1952)

Bulldog Drummond

From The Bulldog Drummond Series By H. C. McNeile (Sapper), continued by Gerard Fairlie

A moment or two later Hugh Drummond came in. Slightly under six feet in height, he was broad in proportion. His best friend would not have called him good-looking, but he was the fortunate possessor of that cheerful type of ugliness which inspires immediate confidence in its owner. His nose had never quite recovered from the final one year in the Public Schools Heavy Weights; his mouth was not small. In fact, to be strictly accurate, only his eyes redeemed his face from being what is known in the vernacular as the Frozen Limit.

Deep-set and steady, with eyelashes that many a woman had envied, they showed the man for what he was – a sportsman and a gentleman. And the combination of the two is an unbeatable production.

Sapper, *Bulldog Drummond*

Walter Pidgeon as Bulldog Drummond in *Calling Bulldog Drummond* **(MGM, 1951)**

Captain Hugh Drummond, DSO, MC, late of His Majesty's Royal Loamshires, is a vigorously cheerful man. His residence is at 60a Half Moon Street, telephone Mayfair 1234 – in October 1925 the telephone number was taken over by Selfridges – is staffed by his ex-batman James Denny and Mrs Denny. A finalist in the public schools heavyweight boxing championships, he is an all-round sportsman, a pipe smoker, driver of a 30mph two-seater, and the owner of a small Colt revolver and a 'Son of a Gun' water-squirt pistol. He learnt the art of undetectable tracking from a Dutch trapper, Van Dyck. A Japanese, Olaki, taught him to kill a man with his bare hands. Drummond practised these skills in his spare time while serving as a platoon commander in France. His mysterious nocturnal wanderings from the trenches often preceded the discovery of a dead German soldier with no wound but a broken neck. These discreet acts of courage were noted by his men who worshipped him.

After his demobilization in 1918 he alleviates the boredom of peacetime by inserting the following advertisement in a newspaper, the extract is from *Bulldog Drummond*.

'Demobilized officer, finding peace incredibly tedious, would welcome diversion. Legitimate if possible; but crime, if of a comparatively humorous description, no objection. Excitement essential. Would be prepared to consider permanent job if suitably impressed by applicant for his services. Reply at once to Box X10.'

One of the many replies comes from a mystery lady who plans a tea-time rendezvous at the Carlton. For identification he is to wear a white flower in his buttonhole. Drummond keeps the appointment and finds she is a pretty young girl, Phyllis Benton. She believes her father to be in danger from a gang of thieves and murderers led by the diabolically clever Carl Peterson, who is plotting the overthrow of Britain. She fears they may have a hold over her father and are using him for their own ends. Drummond eagerly agrees to champion her, and goes into action with the help of three staunch friends, Toby Sinclair, VC, Ted Jerningham, crack shot and master of disguise, and Jerry Seymour of the Flying Corps. After some tough skirmishes with the enemy the courage and determination of the four chums

Left to right David Tomlinson, Peggy Evans and Walter Pidgeon (Bulldog Drummond) in *Calling Bulldog Drummond* **(MGM, 1951)**

wins through. Phyllis's father is saved and the gang is routed – all except Carl Peterson and moll Irma – and Drummond and Phyllis are married. While the happy pair are honeymooning an anonymous note is slipped to Drummond. It reads, 'Only *au revoir*, my friend; only *au revoir*.' It is a challenge thrown down by Carl Peterson. Drummond and his friends are quick to meet it. It takes some time and many adventures before Drummond finally disposes of Peterson (who is blown up in his own airship, designed to assist him in his scheme for world domination). After Peterson's death Drummond finds it hard to kick the habit of crime fighting and many more villains are doomed to face the fearsome four, and eventually bite the dust.

In 1919 the first Bulldog Drummond book was published. The author was newly retired Lieutenant-Colonel Herman Cyril McNeile (Sapper) and the subtitle 'The Adventures of a Demobilised Officer Who Found Peace Dull' probably speaks volumes.

Drummond's blatantly unsubtle methods of dealing with murderers, thieves and other enemies of the British Empire (especially foreigners) found instant popularity with ex-servicemen of World War I but have since been criticized as racist and unnecessarily violent. It is interesting to note the parallel with the American post-World War II writer, Mickey Spillane.

McNeile, the son of Captain Malcolm McNeile, RN, was born in 1888. He was educated at Cheltenham and the Royal Military Academy, Woolwich. He joined the Royal Engineers in 1907 (known as the 'sappers', hence his pseudonym) and served with them for twelve years. In 1914 he was made a lieutenant and by the time of his retirement in 1919 was a lieutenant-colonel. He began to write stories during World War I, although Drummond did not appear until 1919.

Bulldog Drummond is generally supposed to be based on Gerard Fairlie, a friend of McNeile who collaborated with him on some of the 'Drummond' books and plays and eventually took over the writing of them (his first book was *Bulldog Drummond on Dartmoor*). In 1937, while working with Fairlie on the play *Bulldog Drummond Again*, McNeile died at his home in Pulborough, Sussex, of an illness which stemmed from his wartime experiences. He was forty-nine. After his death Fairlie continued to write the 'Drummond' books.

Ian Fleming claimed that the Drummond stories, read to him as a boy, sowed the first seeds of his creation, James Bond, hero of the 1960s.

Publications and Performances

Published texts

Bulldog Drummond. London: Hodder & Stoughton, 1920; New York: Geo H. Doran, 1920.

The Black Gang. London: Hodder & Stoughton, 1922; New York: Geo H. Doran, 1922.

43

The Third Round (title in USA *Bulldog Drummond's Third Round*). London: Hodder & Stoughton, 1924; New York: Geo H. Doran, 1924.

The Final Count. London: Hodder & Stoughton, 1926; New York: Geo H. Doran, 1926.

Female of the Species. London: Hodder & Stoughton, 1928; New York: Doubleday Doran, 1928.

Temple Tower. London: Hodder & Stoughton, 1929; New York: Doubleday Doran, 1929.

Return of Bulldog Drummond (title in USA *Bulldog Drummond Returns*). London: Hodder & Stoughton, 1932; New York: Doubleday Doran, 1932.

Knock-out (title in USA *Bulldog Drummond Strikes Back*). London: Hodder & Stoughton, 1933; New York: Doubleday Doran, 1933.

Bulldog Drummond at Bay. London: Hodder & Stoughton, 1935; New York: Doubleday Doran, 1935.

Challenge. London: Hodder & Stoughton, 1937; New York: Doubleday Doran, 1937.

Bulldog Drummond on Dartmoor (based on a story by 'Sapper' and written by Gerard Fairlie). London: Hodder & Stoughton, 1938; Clue Club Mystery, Hillman Curl, 1939.

Books written by Gerard Fairlie, all published by Hodder & Stoughton: *Bulldog Drummond Attacks*, 1939; *Captain Bulldog Drummond*, 1945; *Bulldog Drummond Stands Fast*, 1947; *Hands off Bulldog Drummond*, 1949; *Calling Bulldog Drummond*, 1951.

On film

Bulldog Drummond. Astra National/Hollandia Film, 1922. Carlyle Blackwell as Drummond.

Bulldog Drummond's Third Round. Astra National, 1925. Jack Buchanan as Drummond.

Bulldog Drummond. Goldwyn/United Artists, 1929. Ronald Colman as Drummond.

Return of Bulldog Drummond. Wardour Films, 1934. Ralph Richardson as Drummond.

Bulldog Drummond Strikes Back. 20th Century Fox, 1934. Ronald Colman as Drummond.

Bulldog Drummond Escapes. Paramount, 1936. Ray Milland as Drummond.

Bulldog Drummond at Bay. Wardour/BIP, 1937. John Lodge as Drummond.

Bulldog Drummond Comes Back, 1937; *Bulldog Drummond in Africa*, 1938; *Bulldog Drummond's Bride*, 1938; *Bulldog Drummond's Peril*, 1938; *Bulldog Drummond's Revenge*, 1938; *Bulldog Drummond's Secret Police*, 1939. All made by Paramount. All starring John Howard as Drummond.

Bulldog Drummond at Bay. Columbia, 1947. Ron Randell as Drummond.

Bulldog Strikes Back. Columbia, 1947. Ron Randell as Drummond.

Calling Bulldog Drummond. MGM, 1951. Walter Pidgeon as Drummond.

Deadlier Than the Male. Rank, 1966. Richard Johnson as Drummond.

Some Girls Do. Rank, 1968. Richard Johnson as Drummond.

In the theatre

Bulldog Drummond by 'Sapper'. Wyndham's Theatre, London, 1921. Gerald Du Maurier as Drummond.

Bulldog Drummond Hits Out by 'Sapper' and Gerard Fairlie. People's Palace, London, July 1937. Jack Allen as Drummond.

Bulldog Drummond Hits Out. Savoy Theatre, London, December 1937. Henry Edwards as Drummond.

Bulldog Drummond Hits Out. 'Q' Theatre, 1938. Wallace Geoffrey as Drummond.

THE HEYDAY

an Carmichael as Lord Peter Wimsey
n *The Nine Tailors* (BBC Television,
974)

Rin Tin Tin in *Frozen River*, the first Rin
Tin Tin sound film (in which he was heard to
bark), starring Nena Quantaro, David Lee
and Raymond McKee (Warner Bros, 1929)

The disaster-laden 1920s and 30s may have looked unpromising for most but for the writers of crime fiction it was to be a bumper period. World War I had resulted in bitter disillusionment, with thousands killed and maimed in ill-managed and meaningless campaigns. The victorious allies straggled home to find unemployment, the depression and economic ruin. The Americans attempted to forget their troubles by making life into one colossal and desperate party flowing with whisky and cocktails. As a result, President Wilson enforced Prohibition in 1920, providing hitherto undreamed-of opportunities for bootleggers, blackmailers and protection racketeers. There was corruption in high places, the collapse of law and order, and an outbreak of violent and bloody gangsterism. Against so suitable a backdrop, American crime fiction reached the peak of its popularity and entered its own golden age.

The new convention of disposable mass-produced cars, and the mindless use of machine guns and automatic pistols, were a gift to the crime genre although Dashiell Hammett, one of the greatest of crime writers, attacked in his novels the spread of violence and corruption in America, as did Chester Gould in his popular comic strip *Dick Tracy*.

But it was not only America that produced an abundance of crime-writing talent in this era. In Britain the Edwardian Arcadia had vanished in a wave of widespread poverty and unemployment which led to the General Strike of 1926. Detective writers such as Agatha Christie and Dorothy L. Sayers provided an opiate of brilliantly constructed puzzles in nostalgically elegant settings.

In the thirties one modern invention was to have more influence on the popularity of fictional sleuths than any other – the cinema Talking pictures augmented the sleuth boom by transferring countless detectives to the silver screen, introducing them to thousands of new fans.

Humphrey Bogart as Philip Marlowe in
The Big Sleep (United Artists, 1946)

Albert Finney (centre) as Hercule Poirot
n *Murder on the Orient Express* with
Martin Balsam and Richard Widmark
EMI, 1974)

Hercule Poirot

From **The Poirot Book Series** By **Agatha Christie**

Poirot was an extraordinary looking little man. He was hardly more than five feet, four inches, but carried himself with great dignity. His head was exactly the shape of an egg, and he always perched it a little on one side. His moustache was very stiff and military. The neatness of his attire was almost incredible, I believe a speck of dust would have caused him more pain than a bullet wound. Yet this quaint dandyfied little man who, I was sorry to see, now limped badly, had been in his time one of the most celebrated members of the Belgian police. As a detective his flair had been extraordinary, and he had achieved triumphs by unravelling some of the most baffling cases of the day.

Agatha Christie, *The Mysterious Affair at Styles*

Albert Finney as Poirot with Lauren Bacall in *Murder on the Orient Express* (EMI, 1974)

The concise little man with hair and moustache so black as to look unnatural, and an obsession for symmetry in everything, is called Hercule Poirot and is often mistaken for a Frenchman although he is in fact a Belgian. Although apparently the most precise of detectives, he does not rely on the accuracy of cold fact in his work. Collecting evidence such as fingerprints, specimens of mud or cigarette ash is merely the means to an end as is stated in *The Murder on the Links*:

The trained observer, the expert, without doubt he is useful! But the others, the Hercule Poirots, they are above the experts. To them the experts bring the facts, their business is the method of the crime, its logical deduction, the proper sequence and order of the facts, above all the true psychology of the case.

Poirot's fanatical love of order makes it impossible for him to tolerate even a hint of asymmetry anywhere, and he cannot resist the impulse to straighten another man's tie or a woman's brooch or complain bitterly because his bread is unevenly toasted.

Never bothered by a little deception in the right place, he keeps his hair and moustache shiny black with dye (later in life he uses a wig and false whiskers). In *Curtain* Poirot shows impatience with the English determination to 'play the game' even when a life is at stake:

Very well, then. You will not look through keyholes. You will remain the English gentleman and someone will be killed. It does not matter, that. Honour comes first with an Englishman. Your honour is more important than somebody else's life. *Bien!* It is understood.

He wastes no time on false modesty, he knows that he is a great detective and expects others to accept the fact as naturally as he does. His Gallic temperament is irrepressible when he is excited by a fresh discovery, and a close observer might also note how green his eyes become at these times.

He started his career as a policeman in Belgium and became one of the most respected detectives in that country. During World War I he was refugeed to Styles St Mary in England. Here he renewed acquaintance with an old friend, Captain Arthur Hastings, invalided home from the front. The reunion involved him in a murder case which he successfully solved. After this he set up as a private detective in London, sharing lodgings with Captain Hastings. He becomes successful enough to be considered fashionable. When the captain marries and goes to live in the Argentine, Poirot moves to the country with his manservant George, and he attempts to retire and grow vegetable marrows. He is completely unsuccessful at retiring but finds himself continuing to be successful at detecting. Eventually doctors order him to Egypt for his health. But there he is once again unable to resist the challenge of a case. On returning his attention is taken by several murders which, he deduces, have all been committed by the same person. His attempts to solve the mystery lead him back to his old haunts of Styles St Mary and another reunion with his old friend Captain Hastings. Now an old man and aware that he has not much longer to live, Poirot shoots the murderer to prevent further killings and allows himself to die, leaving the loose ends to be tidied up by his friend Hastings.

The year 1920 was to prove a milestone in the history of detective fiction, for in this year Agatha Christie made her debut as a crime writer, introduced Hercule Poirot and brought a new approach to the genre. Prior to this, Mrs Christie had published a book of poems and written two or three novels (see the entry on Miss Marple). During

Albert Finney (centre) as Poirot in
Murder on the Orient Express
(EMI, 1974)

Charles Laughton as Poirot in *Alibi* at the Prince of Wales Theatre, London, 1928

World War I she was working with a Voluntary Aid Detachment in Torquay Hospital and it was then that she began to read detective novels, regarding them as 'excellent for taking one's mind off one's worries'. But in her opinion the criminal was easily detectable in all of them, and it occurred to her to try and write one herself which would test her readers' ingenuity. Basing her chief character, M. Poirot, on some of the Belgian refugees she had met and using the knowledge of poisons that her war work had given her, Agatha Christie set about writing *The Mysterious Affair at Styles*.

Popular as M. Poirot became, Mrs Christie was never over-fond of him. She must have agreed with her critics who considered him over-drawn to the point of caricature for, after dispensing with the rather irritating Arthur Hastings early in the series, she toned Poirot down slightly then wrote less and less of him. She killed him in *Curtain*, a book written in the forties but not published until 1975, the year before her own death.

Publications and Performances

Published texts

The Mysterious Affair at Styles, 1920; *The Murder on the Links*, 1923; *Poirot Investigates* (short stories), 1924; *The Murder of Roger Ackroyd*, 1926*; *The Big Four* (short stories), 1927; *Peril at End House*, 1932; *Lord Edgware Dies* (title in USA *Thirteen at Dinner*), 1933*; *Murder on the Orient Express* (title in USA *Murder on the Calais Coach*), 1934*; *Three Act Tragedy* (title in USA *Murder in Three Acts*), 1935*; *The ABC Murders*, 1935*; *Death in the Clouds* (title in USA *Death in the Air*), 1935*; *Murder in Mesopotamia*, 1936*; *Cards on the Table*, 1936; *Dumb Witness* (title in USA *Poirot Loses a Client*), 1937; *Death on the Nile*, 1937*; *Murder in the Mews* (short stories) (title in USA *Dead Man's Mirror*), 1937*; *Appointment with Death*, 1938*; *Hercule Poirot's Christmas* (title in USA *Murder for Christmas*), 1938*; *Sad Cypress*, 1940*; *One, Two, Buckle My Shoe* (title in USA *The Patriotic Murders*), 1940*; *Evil under the Sun*, 1941; *Five Little Pigs* (title in USA *Murder in Retrospect*), 1943; *The Hollow*, 1946; *The Labours of Hercules* (short stories), 1947; *Taken at the Flood* (title in USA *There is a Tide*), 1948*; *Mrs McGinty's Dead*, 1952*; *After the Funeral* (title in USA *Funerals are Fatal*), 1953*; *Hickory Dickory Dock* (title in USA *Hickory Dickory Death*), 1955*; *Dead Man's Folly*, 1956*; *Cat among the Pigeons*, 1959*; *The Adventure of the Christmas Pudding* (Hercule Poirot and Miss Marple short stories), 1960; *The Clocks*, 1963*; *Third Girl*, 1966*; *Hallowe'en Party*, 1969*; *Elephants Can Remember*, 1972; *Poirot's Early Cases* (short stories), 1974; *Curtain*, 1975.
Published in UK by Wm Collins, London; and in USA by Dodd, Mead, New York.

On film

Alibi. Twickenham Films, 1931. Austin Trevor as Hercule Poirot.

Black Coffee. Twickenham Films, 1931. Austin Trevor as Hercule Poirot.

Lord Edgware Dies. RKO Radio, 1934. Austin Trevor as Hercule Poirot.

The Alphabet Murders. MGM, 1965. Tony Randall as Hercule Poirot.

Murder on the Orient Express. EMI, 1974. Albert Finney as Hercule Poirot.

In the theatre

Alibi by Michael Morton. Adapted from *The Murder of Roger Ackroyd*. Prince of Wales Theatre, London, 1928. Charles Laughton as Hercule Poirot.

Black Coffee by Agatha Christie. St Martin's Theatre, London, 1931. Francis L. Sullivan as Hercule Poirot.

Peril at End House. Adapted by Arnold Ridley. Vaudeville Theatre, London, 1940. Francis L. Sullivan as Hercule Poirot.

* Reprinted in Fontana paperbacks, published by Wm Collins, London.

Peter Wimsey

From **The Peter Wimsey Stories** By **Dorothy L. Sayers**

Lord Peter finished a Scarlatti sonata, and sat looking thoughtfully at his own hands. The fingers were long and muscular, with wide, flat joints and square tips. When he was playing, his rather hard grey eyes softened, and his long, indeterminate mouth hardened in compensation. At no other time had he any pretensions to good looks, and at all times he was spoilt by a long, narrow chin, and a long, receding forehead, accentuated by the brushed-back sleekness of his tow-coloured hair. Labour papers, softening down his chin, caricatured him as a typical aristocrat.

Dorothy L. Sayers, *Whose Body?*

Peter Death Bredon Wimsey, DSO, was born in 1890, the younger son of Mortimer Gerald Bredon Wimsey, 15th Duke of Denver. He was educated at Eton College and at Balliol College, Oxford. His school career started badly. His natural fastidiousness prompted the other boys' corruption of his name to 'Flimsey' and he was on his way to becoming the school comedian. But when a games master discovered his talent for cricket he began to command the respect of the school, and by the time he had reached the sixth form he was looked upon as an excellent athlete, scholar and wit, far outshining his older brother

Ian Carmichael as Lord Peter Wimsey with Gwen Taylor in *Murder Must Advertise* (BBC Television, 1973)

Gerald. At this time the duke, who never had much time for Peter, was busy extricating his older son from an awkward tangle up at Oxford. Peter put himself under the wing of his uncle Paul Delgardie who took him to Paris and taught him the finer points of high society. In 1909 Wimsey went up to Balliol with a scholarship to read history. Here he acquired a monocle and a good deal of affectation. His father was killed by a fall from his horse in 1911. Gerald succeeded to the title and married his cousin Helen, who nursed a deep loathing for Peter. The feeling was mutual.

During his last year at Oxford Peter fell in love with a pretty empty-headed girl of seventeen. World War I prevented their

Robert Montgomery as Peter Wimsey in
Busman's Honeymoon **(MGM, 1940)**

The Wimsey coat of arms devised by C. W. Scott Giles, Fitzalan Pursuivant, College of Arms, London

I HOLD BY MY WHIMSY

marriage. Peter served as a captain in the Rifle Brigade. Returning home on leave he found his sweetheart married to another and returned to the front hoping to be killed. He was made a major, received the DSO for his intelligence work behind the enemy lines and was blown up and buried in a shell hole. The result was a nervous breakdown lasting two years, after which he bought a flat in Piccadilly and lived there with Bunter, his devoted ex-sergeant, as his valet.

In 1922 Wimsey was chief witness for the prosecution in the case of the Attenbury emeralds. This was the beginning of his involvement with criminology. He made a friend of Charles Parker of Scotland Yard, who later married his sister. His reputation as a detective began to grow until criminology became more than just a hobby, although at the end of each case he is tormented by the recurring symptoms of shellshock.

Bunter, a skilled and enthusiastic photographer, becomes Lord Peter's right-hand man.

When his brother is indicted on a murder charge, Lord Peter wins the case for him. He also clears the name of novelist Harriet Vane, accused of murdering her lover, falls in love, and seven years later, when he is forty-five, marries her.

Apart from criminology his hobbies include bibliography, cricket and music. He is author of several books relating to his hobbies. His clubs are Marlborough and Egoists. His country residence is Bredon Hall, Dukes Denver in Norfolk, and 110 Piccadilly in town.

Agatha Christie wrote her first detective novel in 1920, but success on a large scale did not reach her until 1926. Between these two dates Dorothy L. Sayers, with perfect timing, wrote her first Peter Wimsey book and just beat Mrs Christie to the 'Queen of Crime' title.

Peter Wimsey and his manservant Bunter have often been compared with P. G. Wodehouse's Bertie Wooster and Jeeves. Peter Wimsey and Bertie Wooster are both aristocratic young men-about-town, both speak with a nonchalant upper-class drawl (so earnestly strived after by Philo Vance [qv] – who is always compared with Peter Wimsey) and both were admirably portrayed on British television by Ian Carmichael. But Bertie Wooster really *is* a drivelling ass, while Peter Wimsey only appears to be – sometimes. Jeeves and Bunter are both confidential manservants with more than their share of native cunning. But Jeeves is brighter than his master and Bunter, in the long run, isn't.

The deceptive Lord Peter is a most suitable instrument for the conveyance of Miss Sayers' intricate plots. From the purposely languid in *Five Red Herrings*: 'After all, if anybody did do the poor devil in, it's rather up to one to get it detected, and so on', to hidden dynamite in the same book: 'You don't know me. I could get away from a galloping fire engine' – the progressions of a Wimsey investigation are fascinating to watch.

Dorothy L. Sayers was born in East Anglia, the daughter of the Rev H. Sayers, one-time headmaster of the Cathedral Choir School, Oxford. In 1915 she obtained a first honours degree in medieval literature and was one of the first women to hold an Oxford degree. Her first 'Peter Wimsey' book was *Whose Body?* published in 1923. Peter Wimsey brought her a fame which she was at great pains to avoid claiming, Garbo-like, that her private life was just that. In 1926 she married Captain Oswald Atherton Fleming, and towards the end of her life wrote less and less crime. Her controversial radio play, *The Man Born to be King* (it was the first radio play in which an actor portrayed Christ) was revived in 1975 and pronounced harmless.

This highly individual lady left behind her a reputation which leans to the eccentric. After gaining her degree she joined Benson's advertising agency as a £4 a week copywriter (Colman's Mustard being one of the most successful promotions she worked on), she chain-smoked and liked to wear suits, silk blouses, tie and cuff-links.

She was a prolific writer. Besides her detective novels she wrote verse, plays, religious works and was an anthologist of detective fiction.

She died of a coronary thrombosis on 17 December 1957.

Publications and Performances

Selected published texts

Whose Body? London: Ernest Benn, 1923; New York: Boni & Liveright, 1923.

Clouds of Witness. London: Ernest Benn, 1926; New York: McVeagh, 1927.

Unnatural Death (title in USA *The Dawson Pedigree*). London: Ernest Benn, 1927; London: Victor Gollancz, 1927; New York: McVeagh, 1928.

Unpleasantness at the Bellona Club. London: Ernest Benn, 1928; New York: Payson & Clark, 1928.

Lord Peter Views the Body. London: Victor Gollancz, 1929; New York: F. R. Brewer, 1929.

Strong Poison. London: Victor Gollancz, 1930; New York: F. R. Brewer, 1930.

Five Red Herrings (title in USA *Suspicious Characters*). London: Victor Gollancz, 1931; New York: Harcourt, Brace, 1931.

Have His Carcass. London: Victor Gollancz, 1932; New York: F. R. Brewer, 1932.

Murder Must Advertise. London: Victor Gollancz, 1933; New York: Harcourt, Brace, 1933.

Hangman's Holiday. London: Victor Gollancz, 1933; New York: Harcourt, Brace, 1933.

Nine Tailors. London: Victor Gollancz, 1934; New York: Harcourt, Brace, 1934.

Gaudy Night. London: Victor Gollancz, 1935; New York: Harcourt, Brace, 1936.

Busman's Honeymoon. London: Victor Gollancz, 1937; New York: Harcourt, Brace, 1937.

In the Teeth of the Evidence. London: Victor Gollancz, 1939; New York: Harcourt, Brace, 1940.

All of the above titles reprinted in New English Library paperbacks.

New Sayers Omnibus. London: Victor Gollancz, 1956.

Lord Peter Omnibus. London: Victor Gollancz, 1964.

On film

The Silent Passenger. ABFD Pathé, 1935. Peter Hadden as Peter Wimsey.

Busman's Honeymoon (title in USA *Haunted Honeymoon*). MGM 1940. Robert Montgomery as Peter Wimsey.

In the theatre

Busman's Honeymoon, adapted by Dorothy L. Sayers and M. St Clare Byrne, Comedy Theatre, London, 1936. Denis Arundell as Peter Wimsey.

Television

Between 1970 and 1975 BBC Television produced serialized versions of five of the Peter Wimsey stories, *Murder Must Advertise*; *Unpleasantness at the Bellona Club*; *Clouds of Witness*; *The Nine Tailors*; *Five Red Herrings*. Ian Carmichael as Peter Wimsey.

Rin Tin Tin

From **The Film Series** By **Warner Brothers Studios**

Rin Tin Tin is the dog who is everyone's idea of man's best friend –
faithful, courageous, intelligent and strong. His life is spent in the
service of his master, or rather masters, for Rinty has a disconcerting
habit of changing them frequently – usually after they've married the
girl of their dreams. But this dog is not just another intrepid hound,
his efforts have sent many villains to their rightful end. He seems to
attract masters with a penchant for getting themselves into trouble
with the blackest of scoundrels, and it is usually left to our hero dog
not only to extricate his luckless owner from their clutches but to
track down the rogues and bring them to justice. In 1927, for instance,
the engineer of a big dam construction fell ill. His junior (Rinty's
master) took over from the old man, at the same time falling in love
with his daughter. The corrupt foreman and his gang planned to
wreck the works by opening the sluice gates. Rin Tin Tin thwarted
their plans by pulling the lever with his teeth and tracking the villains
to their eventual downfall, saving his master from a gunshot wound
and the girl from death in the raging torrent.

In the same year he could be found working as a Red Cross

Rin Tin Tin and Jason Robards in *Jaws of
Steel* **(Warner Bros, 1927)**

Hospital dog when he managed to save the life of an American airman captured by Germans. He achieved one of his greatest triumphs when cast ashore with his master near a lighthouse the very night that the light must be kept burning by the blind lighthouse-keeper to trap smugglers. The villains invaded the lighthouse and were in danger of winning, but Rinty (having brushed aside the attack of their savage bulldog) saved everyone else and lit the light with a torch set by his master's unbound feet (the rogues having bound him hand but not foot) thereby causing the capture of the villains and leaving his master free to marry the lighthouse-keeper's daughter.

There are no regulations which state the number of legs allowed a sleuth, and Rin Tin Tin's instinct for catching villains and spies and busting gangs wide open qualifies him as a genuine canine Bulldog Drummond. Known affectionately as 'the mortgage lifter' by his studio, Warner Brothers, Rin Tin Tin was one of the animals who, it has been claimed, was happy in his work and there is certainly no concrete evidence to prove the contrary.

His official biography reads like the plot of a film itself. On 15 September 1918, Corporal Lee Duncan was with a small party of enlisted men searching for a new field site for 136th Aero Squadron. They came across a badly shelled and abandoned war dog station. In the mud of a blasted dugout they discovered a shivering starving bitch with her five puppies. They rescued the animals and when the war was over Duncan brought two of them home. He called them Nanette and Rin Tin Tin after the mascots carried by French soldiers and airmen. Nanette died of pneumonia during the journey, but Rinty survived to become a multimillion-dollar star with his own production unit, valet, chef and chauffeur (with private limousine). Not that he didn't work for his (or rather Warner Brothers') money. Over the years, from the time he was spotted as an extra playing a wolf, he jumped, climbed, swam and crawled through, over, under and around more obstacles than can bear counting. He probably posed for as many pictures as Mary Pickford and sat still for hours while they lit the tricky black patches on his head and back. He sired a healthy litter of puppies one of which followed in father's paw-prints and became an actor.

He died at the age of fourteen while playing with Duncan in the front garden of their Beverly Hills home. Jean Harlow, their near neighbour, saw that something was wrong and ran across the street. She and Duncan held Rin Tin Tin in their arms as he passed away.

A suitably moral epilogue to the Rin Tin Tin story is provided by an earlier quote from Duncan when asked why he had saved the family of dogs from certain death in France. If you listen carefully, you can hear the background music:

It was my mother, I am sure. Like I heard her voice even out there. When I was a kid she always reminded me to be kind to animals. She said 'A boy who loves animals can love people twice as much.'

Performances

On film

Where the North Begins, 1923; *Lighthouse by the Sea*, 1924; *Clash of the Wolves*, 1924; *While London Sleeps*, 1926; *Night Cry*, 1926; *Tracked by the Police*, 1927; *Jaws of Steel*, 1927; *Dog of the Regiment*, 1927; *Frozen River* ('talkie', in which Rin Tin Tin was heard to bark), 1929; *Man Hunter*, 1930.
    All films produced by Warner Brothers.
    A number of Rin Tin Tin films were produced between 1923 and 1932 by Warner Brothers, but details of many of them tend to be inconsistent.

In the theatre

Personal appearance tours in 1923, 1926 and 1930.

Charlie Chan

From **The Charlie Chan Book Series** By **Earl Derr Biggers**

He was very fat indeed, yet he walked with the light dainty step of a woman. His cheeks were as chubby as a baby's, his skin ivory tinted, his black hair close-cropped, his amber eyes slanting. As he passed Miss Minerva he bowed with a courtesy encountered all too rarely in a work-a-day world . . .

Earl Derr Biggers, *The House without a Key*

You could call Inspector Charles Chan of the Honolulu police 'lovable' or even 'cuddly', but you would be doing a considerable injustice to his Oriental dignity and self-respect. Mr Chan is a large Chinaman who lives up to the popularly inscrutable image of his people. Speaking Cantonese only when necessary, he strives to master the English language in its purest form – anything less being an affront to his poetically precise ideals. Any lapse such as the occasional 'hot dog' or 'see you later' is explained as the unfortunate influence of his cousin Willie Chan, captain of the all-Chinese baseball team. His eleven children are educated to speak American-English which pains him greatly. They are more inclined to worship film stars than ancestors and find their father's refined Oriental ideals unspeakably outdated. Mrs Chan is a jolly woman, nearly as large as her husband. She remains firmly Chinese. In the aggressive hustle of police life

Warner Oland as Charlie Chan (right) in *Charlie Chan Carries On* **(20th Century Fox, 1930)**

Warner Oland as Charlie Chan in
Charlie Chan in Shanghai **(20th Century Fox, 1935)**

Charlie Chan, in *The House without a Key*, remains imperturbably patient, calm and polite: 'You will do me the great honour to accompany me to the station, if you please.' Following the Chinese tradition, he is self-deprecating and apologetic. None of which stops him from quietly and efficiently getting his man.

Part of his method is to single out and follow through one essential clue. But most of his work is based on the study of 'human people', as he states in *The House without a Key*:

> Finger-prints and other mechanics good in books, in real life not so much so. My experience tell me to think deep about human people. Human passions. Back of murder what, always? Hate, revenge, need to make silent the slain one. Greed for money, maybe. Study human people at all times.

Chan started his working life in Honolulu as a 'boy' in a large house on the beach. He left to join the police force where he made a good record for himself, was promoted to detective-sergeant and later to inspector.

His home is a bungalow built on the side of Punchbowl Hill affording a panoramic view of his beloved and exotically beautiful Honolulu. Although he is sometimes frustrated by the lack of crime on the island, his visits to other places have made him appreciate the calm delights of island life.

He is modest about his personal success but in *The House without a Key* he shows his pride in his heritage, which he believes gives him his powers of detection: 'Chinese most psychic people in the world. Sensitives, like film in camera. A look, a laugh, a gesture perhaps. Something go click.' 'Something go click' very often for Charlie Chan.

Harvard graduate, novelist and ex-journalist Earl Derr Biggers, a dark, round, little man with twinkling eyes, must have been as pleasant and likeable as his gentle creation Charlie Chan. As a journalist he ran a humorous column for the Boston *Traveler*, the writing of which, he was later to comment, was a good deal like making faces in church – it offended a lot of nice people, and it wasn't much fun.

Although the fame of Charlie Chan has outlived his creator (Biggers died of a heart disease in 1933 while still in his early forties), the Charlie Chan books themselves tend to be overlooked today, although they are as readable now as ever and the flavour of the 1920s and 30s can be enjoyed as 'period' rather than scorned as 'outdated'.

The dignity of Charlie Chan is Earl Derr Biggers' gentle protest for the identity of the Chinaman in the America of those days, which he articulates in *Charlie Chan Carries On*: 'We are not highly valued in the United States, where we are appraised as laundrymen, or maybe villains in the literature of the talkative films.' Such was the talent of Earl Derr Biggers that in spite of Chan's quaint accent and cuddly ways he was a character that engendered respect very much as the author himself must have done, I imagine.

Publications and Performances

Published texts

The House without a Key. New York: Bobbs, Merrill, 1925; London: Harrap, 1926.

The Chinese Parrot. New York: Bobbs, Merrill, 1926; London: Harrap, 1927.

Behind That Curtain. New York: Bobbs, Merrill,1928; London: Harrap,1928.

Black Camel. New York: Bobbs, Merrill, 1929; London: Cassell, 1930.

Charlie Chan Carries On. New York: Bobbs, Merrill, 1930; London: Cassell, 1931.

Keeper of the Keys. New York: Bobbs, Mcrrill, 1932; London: Cassell, 1932.

The Charlie Chan Omnibus ('The House without a Key', 'Behind that Curtain', and 'Keeper of the Keys'). New York: Grosset & Dunlap, 1932.

Celebrated Cases of Charlie Chan. New York: Bobbs, Merrill, 1933; London: Cassell, 1933.

On film

House without a Key (10-part serial). Pathé, 1926. George Kuwa as Charlie Chan.

A version of the *Chinese Parrot* was made in 1928, starring the Japanese actor Sojin as Charlie Chan, but no prints of this production appear to exist.

Behind That Curtain. 20th Century Fox, 1929. E. L. Park as Charlie Chan.

Charlie Chan Carries On. 20th Century Fox, 1930. The first of sixteen films made by 20th Century Fox starring Warner Oland as Charlie Chan, among them: *Charlie Chan's Chance*, 1931; *Charlie Chan's Greatest Case*, 1933; *Charlie Chan's Courage* (from *The Chinese Parrot*), 1934; *Charlie Chan in Shanghai*, 1935; *Charlie Chan at the Race Track*, 1936; *Charlie Chan at Monte Carlo*, 1936; *Charlie Chan at the Opera*, 1937; *Charlie Chan on Broadway*, 1937.

After Warner Oland's death in 1938 the role was assumed by Sidney Toler who made, amongst others: *Charlie Chan in Reno*, 1939; *Charlie Chan in City of Darkness*, 1939; *Charlie Chan's Murder Cruise*, 1940; *Charlie Chan at the Wax Museum*, 1940; *Charlie Chan in the Secret Service*, 1943; *Black Magic*, 1944. All films produced by 20th Century Fox.

Sidney Toler was followed, in 1947, by Roland Winters who made six films for Monogram Pictures beginning with *The Chinese Ring* in 1947, and ending with *Sky Dragon* in 1949.

Television

The New Adventures of Charlie Chan. ITC Productions, 1957–8. J. Carroll Naish as Charlie Chan.

There is no record of any theatre production featuring Charlie Chan.

Sidney Toler as Charlie Chan with Sen Yung as Jimmy Chan in *Charlie Chan at the Wax Museum* (20th Century Fox, 1940)

J. G. Reeder

From The Book Series By Edgar Wallace

Mr Reeder was something over fifty, a long-faced gentleman with sandy-grey hair and a slither of side whiskers that mercifully distracted attention from his large outstanding ears. He wore halfway down his nose a pair of steel-rimmed pince-nez, through which nobody had ever seen him look – they were invariably removed when he was reading. A high and flat-crowned bowler hat matched and yet did not match a frock-coat tightly buttoned across his sparse chest. His boots were square-toed, his cravat – of the broad, chest-protector pattern – was ready-made and buckled into place behind a Gladstone collar. The neatest appendage to Mr Reeder was an umbrella rolled so tightly that it might be mistaken for a frivolous walking cane. Rain or shine, he carried this article hooked to his arm, and within living memory it had never been unfurled.

Edgar Wallace, *The Mind of Mr J. G. Reeder*

A tentative man with tightly rolled umbrella, pince-nez and bowler hat is the music-hall version of the eternal civil servant. As an investigator attached to the Public Prosecutor's Office, J. G. Reeder is technically in the civil service. On first acquaintance Mr Reeder, nervously apologetic, fastidious, unemotional and lacking in humour, would seem to fit the popular, if unfair, image of that profession and further acquaintance does not inspire confidence, rather more pity. Yet Mr Reeder seems unconscious of either derision or pity. Self-sufficiency is his strength. In *Red Aces* we learn just how foreign emotional involvement is to him: 'I know so very little – um – about love,' said Mr Reeder awkwardly, 'In fact – er – nothing.' It is difficult to say if he misses the comforting intimacies of a close friendship, a love affair or a marriage. Probably not.

Will Fyffe (centre) as J. G. Reeder in *The Mind of Mr Reeder* (Grand National, 1939)

As a private detective, Mr Reeder became an expert in the field of forgery, working for the Bank of England before his appointment to the Public Prosecutor's Office (an appointment he is none too sure about, being 'suspicious of all government departments'). His fame is international in the criminal world. He can recite detailed accounts of most crimes and criminals in the business and he is aware of the many vendettas held against him. The general public, on the whole, know the name. His colleagues appreciate him once they have experienced him. His reticence (his bland ways so irritatingly uncommunicative) and his infuriating habit of being gently right keeps him one step ahead, as may be seen in *Red Aces*:

'But how do you know they're diaries?' demanded the police officer testily.

'Because the word "diary" is printed on the inside covers,' said Mr Reeder, more gently than ever.

Mr Reeder is not one of the great analytical detectives, his talent is for observation and, having observed, connecting the links of his observations. He has the ability to listen. The art of listening, he believes, is the art of detection and those who don't know and think him harmless find him easy to talk to. His own theory (expounded in *Red Aces*) regarding his success is simple: 'I have a criminal mind. I see the worst in people and the worst in every human action. It is very tragic.'

His occasional short, sharp outbursts of impatience are unexpected and almost shocking in contrast with his usual impassiveness. Equally unexpected are his moments of quiet sympathy and kindliness. Contrary to general opinion he is not immune to a pretty face, but he is always the soul of propriety, easily embarrassed. Sometimes he has been seen to blush.

As befits a respectable elderly gentleman he lives in a well-ordered house in Brockley Road, watched over by a resident housekeeper and a small daily staff. His hobby is poultry, about which he knows a great deal. He owns a chicken farm in Kent and has been consulted on the subject by the highest in the land.

Perhaps the saddest thing about J. G. Reeder is the quiet melancholy which underlines all he says and does. By definition a detective cannot be all quietness, however. His neighbours in Brockley would be amazed could they see the long-barrelled Browning automatic nestling under his coat. And as for the eternally rolled umbrella, a swordstick may be old-fashioned but it has its uses. And what of the sense of humour generally known to be so lacking in him? Perhaps we learn something of this in *Red Aces*:

'You always keep back some juicy bit to spring on us at the last moment. It's either your sense of drama or your sense of humour.' For a moment Reeder's eyes twinkled and then his face became a mask again. 'I have no – um – sense of humour,' he said.

A 1932 cover of *The Thriller* magazine featuring a J. G. Reeder story

When it comes to popular crime novelists they don't come much more popular than Edgar Wallace, who is regarded as having been the most prolific pop writer of his or any other day. In 1928 it was reckoned that (excluding Bibles and textbooks) every fourth book printed and sold in England was an Edgar Wallace.

His early experience as a racing journalist, a crime reporter and Reuter's second correspondent in Cape Town, probably all combined to give him his facility for speedy crime fiction – he certainly had a good, and obviously authentic, 1920s underworld vocabulary.

He once dictated an entire novel between Friday night and Monday morning. This may be good material for *The Guinness Book of*

Opening chapter of *The Shadow Man*
from *The Thriller*, **30 January 1932**

Records, but does not always result in good fiction, pop or otherwise, and much of Wallace's work has been dismissed as slapdash and two dimensional. J. G. Reeder is recognized as his most appealing and enduring creation, but there is no material evidence to prove that Wallace spent any more time on him than he did on any of the others.

Publications and Performances

Published texts

Room 13. London: John Long, 1924.

The Mind of Mr J. G. Reeder (title in USA *Murder Book of Mr Reeder*). London: Hodder & Stoughton, 1925; New York: Doubleday, Doran, 1929.

Terror Keep. London: Hodder & Stoughton, 1927; New York: Doubleday, Doran, 1927.

Red Aces. London: Hodder & Stoughton, 1929; New York: Doubleday, Doran, 1931.

The Guv'nor and other Stories (title in USA *Mr Reeder Returns*). London: Collins, 1932; New York: Doubleday, Doran, 1932.

The Crime Book of J. G. Reeder (containing 'Terror Keep', 'Red Aces' and 'Mr Reeder Returns'). New York: A. L. Burt, 1935.

Mr J. G. Reeder Returns. London: Hodder & Stoughton, 1965.

On film

Mr Reeder in Room 13. British National, 1938. Gibb McLaughlin as Mr J. G. Reeder.

Mind of Mr Reeder and *Missing People*. Grand National, 1939. Will Fyffe as Mr J. G. Reeder.

Television

The Mind of Mr Reeder. Thames Television, 1972. Hugh Burden as Mr J. G. Reeder.

There is no record of any theatre production featuring Mr J. G. Reeder.

Philo Vance

From **The Book Series** By **S. S. Van Dine**

Vance was a marked Nordic type, with a long, sharply chiselled face; grey, wide set eyes; a narrow aquiline nose; and a straight oval chin. His mouth, too, was firm and clean-cut, but it held a look of cynical cruelty which was more Mediterranean than Nordic. His face was strong and attractive, though not exactly handsome. It was the face of a thinker and recluse; and its very severity – at once studious and introspective – acted as a barrier between him and his fellows.

S. S. Van Dine, *The Bishop Murder Case*

Paul Lukas as Philo Vance with Louise Fazenda in *The Casino Murder Case* (MGM, 1935)

It was at Harvard, where he was 'the bane of his professors and the fear of his fellow classmen' that Philo Vance first met S. S. Van Dine who was later to become his legal adviser, constant companion and chronicler. After spells at Harvard and Oxford, Vance inherited a vast fortune from a deceased aunt. He returned from Europe, where he had been living, and, the transaction of business matters being distasteful to him, offered Van Dine the post of general custodian of his financial affairs. He was now free to devote his extraordinarily rarefied intellect to the study of art in all its forms. To say that art is his passion would be misleading for Vance is a peculiarly passionless man. He prefers to remain aloof from the rest of humanity and his culture, brilliance and wealth allows him to do so. A disdainful cynic whose selectivity is 'intellectual as well as social', it is debatable whether he actually thinks of himself as a member of the human race.

His apartment in New York is the beautifully remodelled top two floors of an old mansion in East 38th Street (with roof garden) where he keeps many priceless works of art, his extensive wardrobe, exquisite furniture (including a mother of pearl telephone) and his old English retainer, Currie. He affects an English upper-class drawl, dropping the 'g's at the ends of words, omitting selected vowels and using the contraction ain't. His expletives rarely exceed 'Amazin'!', 'My word!' or 'Most extr'ordin'ry!'. His accomplishments include chess, horse riding (he has ridden to hounds in England), fencing, polo, golf, philosophy, anthropology, Egyptology, biology and so on. He resents expending his energy on anyone or anything beneath his own mental capacity, but if his interest is caught he will give his undivided attention.

A fellow member of the Stuyvesant Club, District Attorney John F. X. Markham, fulfilling a promise, took him along as an observer to an investigation. Vance became fascinated, applied his own theories to the case and, behold, it was solved. He believes that every person is a potential criminal but every mind is individual (a theory that contrasts strangely with his general attitude of disdain towards the human race). Therefore, if only the personal trademark that must invariably be stamped on a crime is found, then so is the criminal. Backed up by scientific knowledge of the highest complexity, this theory makes Vance a detective *par excellence* and, as Markham grudgingly acknowledges, indispensable to the crime-fighters of America – or indeed the world.

Surveyed from a distance, Philo Vance is a cross between Sherlock Holmes and Peter Wimsey and seems to fall sadly between the two. To read every word of a Philo Vance novel from beginning to end can be quite an undertaking for the uninitiated for it is full of Vance's lengthy discourses on the science of crime and one lecture can delay development of the story line for pages at a time. But for the students of crime fiction these books must have been an innovation when they first appeared. Philo Vance is an unbelievably precious know-all who has decided to inflict his genius on the world of crime. As a character study he has little or no substance – for who can believe in a personality built only on a set of gimmicky affectations and the constant airing of intellectual prowess. S. S. Van Dine (pseudonym for Willard Huntingdon Wright) was himself an intellectual dilettante with a great capacity for absorbing new subjects. A literary and art critic he had published a novel and some works on art and philosophy before he started writing detective fiction. He studied crime whilst recovering from a nervous breakdown and communicated his findings through his creation, Philo Vance, adding titbits from many other subjects dear to his heart such as art, ancient history and so forth. As his knowledge was relevant and thorough it lent substance to the otherwise insubstantial Philo Vance.

Van Dine set down his own twenty rules for writing detective novels which he prefaced with his belief that:

> The detective story is a kind of intellectual game. It is more – it is a sporting event. And the author must play fair with the reader. He can no more resort to trickeries and deceptions and still retain his honesty than if he cheated in a game of bridge. He must outwit the reader, and hold the reader's interest through sheer ingenuity.

S. S. Van Dine's honest ingenuity has outwitted many crime buffs fair and square, and made the Van Dine books a landmark in the history of crime fiction.

Publications and Performances

Published texts

The Benson Murder Case. New York: C. Scribner's Sons, 1926; London: Cassell, 1931.

The Canary Murder Case. New York: C. Scribner's Sons, 1927; London: Ernest Benn, 1927.

The Greene Murder Case. New York: C. Scribner's Sons, 1928; London: Ernest Benn, 1928.

The Bishop Murder Case. New York: C. Scribner's Sons, 1929; London: Cassell, 1931.

The Scarab Murder Case. New York: C. Scribner's Sons, 1930; London: Cassell, 1932.

The Kennel Murder Case. New York: C. Scribner's Sons, 1931; London: Cassell, 1931.

The Dragon Murder Case. New York: C. Scribner's Sons, 1933; London: Cassell, 1935.

The Casino Murder Case. New York: C. Scribner's Sons, 1934; London: Cassell, 1934.

The Kidnap Murder Case. New York: C. Scribner's Sons, 1936; London: Cassell, 1936.

The Garden Murder Case. New York: C. Scribner's Sons, 1938; London: Cassell, 1938.

The Gracie Allen Murder Case. New York: C. Scribner's Sons, 1938; London: Cassell, 1938.

The Winter Murder Case. New York: C. Scribner's Sons, 1939; London: Cassell, 1939.

On film

The Canary Murder Case. Paramount, 1929. William Powell as Philo Vance.

The Greene Murder Case. Paramount, 1929. William Powell as Philo Vance.

The Benson Murder Case. Paramount, 1930. William Powell as Philo Vance.

The Bishop Murder Case. MGM, 1930. Basil Rathbone as Philo Vance.

The Kennel Murder Case. Warner Bros, 1933. William Powell as Philo Vance.

The Dragon Murder Case. Warner Bros, 1934. Warren William as Philo Vance.

The Casino Murder Case. MGM, 1935. Paul Lukas as Philo Vance.

The Garden Murder Case. MGM, 1936. Edmund Lowe as Philo Vance.

The Scarab Murder Case. Paramount, 1936. Wilfred Hyde White as Philo Vance.

Night of Mystery (remake of *The Greene Murder Case*). Paramount, 1937. Grant Richards as Philo Vance.

The Gracie Allen Murder Case. Paramount, 1939. Warren Williams as Philo Vance.

Calling Philo Vance (remake of *The Kennel Murder Case*). Warner Bros, 1940. James Stephenson as Philo Vance.

Philo Vance Returns. PRC (Producers Releasing Corporation), 1947. William Wright as Philo Vance.

Philo Vance's Gamble. PRC, 1947. Alan Curtis as Philo Vance.

Philo Vance's Secret Mission. PRC, 1947. Alan Curtis as Philo Vance.

There is no record of a Philo Vance stage production.

Grant Richards as Philo Vance with Roscoe Karns in *Night of Mystery* (Paramount, 1937)

Ellery Queen

From **The Ellery Queen Book Series**
By **Frederic B. Dannay and Manfred B. Lee (pseudonym Ellery Queen)**

Ellery Queen towered six inches above his father's head. There was a square cut to his shoulders and an agreeable swing to his body as he walked. He was dressed in Oxford grey and carried a light stick. On his nose perched what seemed an incongruous note in so athletic a man – a rimless pince-nez. But the brow above, the long, delicate lines of the face, the bright eyes were those of a man of thought rather than action.

Ellery Queen, *The Roman Hat Mystery*

Inspector Richard Queen of the New York Homicide Squad is an astute and thorough policeman, a much-respected executive of the Detective Division. He is a modest man, not given to bullying but very well able to assert himself when necessary. He is a habitual snuff taker and has a collection of valuable antique snuff boxes. He also has a son, Ellery. Ellery has two obsessions in life – books and criminology. These have combined to make him a talented author of crime fiction. He is a compulsive book collector and his collection of works on violence is perhaps one of the most comprehensive in the world. Through his fascination with crime he has involved himself in his father's work and the two men liaise closely on most of the inspector's cases. The value of this merger is appreciated by the police force who afford Ellery as much respect as they do his father.

Inspector Queen is a small man, unassuming and benevolent in appearance but with an impressive dignity. He contrasts oddly with his son who is six inches taller and surprisingly athletic looking for one so studious. The only outward sign of the bibliophile is the rimless pince-nez that Ellery wears and constantly adjusts, removes, replaces, polishes and generally utilizes as an aid to concentration. Superficially Ellery is something of an untidy wretch and his approach to an investigation may seem decidedly casual – particularly if it entails the sacrifice of a book about to be bought or read – but this should fool no one for he has a brain which is precise, ordered and methodical.

Ellery's talents for detection are deductive and analytical, coupled with the intuition and imagination of a fiction writer. They blend perfectly with his father's mastery of methodical investigation. As Richard is the official representative of the team he invariably receives the plaudits. This worries Ellery not one jot. Nevertheless the inspector is always quick to pass the credit to his son. Although their repartee is invariably irascible, their relationship is strong and close. Their apartment on West 87th Street is on the top floor of a house which is 'a relic of late Victorian times'. Their comfortable sitting-room is surrounded by high bookcases and the walls are decorated with two shining sabres and a pipe rack over the hearth. It is furnished liberally with comfortable armchairs and sofas, footstools and bright-coloured leather cushions. In the narrow hallway a tapestry depicting the chase is hung (detested by both the Queens but tolerated as a gift from a grateful client).

Djuna, a sprightly gipsy lad of nineteen, lives with them as their willing and adoring general factotum. An orphan for as long as he can remember, he was taken in by Richard while Ellery was at college.

This splendid trio remains inseparable. When Ellery marries it becomes a quartet and moves to the peace of an Italian mountain-village. Here Ellery becomes, in the *Roman Hat Mystery*, 'the startled father of an infant who resembled his grandfather to an extraordinary degree', and the quintet is as inseparable as the quartet.

Frederic Dannay and Manfred Lee were Brooklyn-born cousins who collaborated under the name of 'Ellery Queen' as authors and anthologists of crime fiction.

Each Ellery Queen novel carries a foreword bearing the initials J. J. McC., a supposedly mysterious friend and confidant of the detectives who persuaded them to release their manuscripts for publishing, having promised that the pseudonyms Ellery and Richard Queen be substituted for their real ones. *The Spanish Cape Mystery* bore a foreword to its foreword, issued by 'the publishers':

> In the course of the five years or so during which we have had the pleasure of publishing Mr. Queen's novels, hundreds of enquiries have been addressed to us demanding an explanation both for the mystery surrounding and the identity of the gentleman who has invariably written the forewords to the Queen books. We regret that we cannot satisfy our correspondents. We do not know.

Jim Hutton (right) as Ellery Queen with David Wayne as Inspector Queen in the MCA *Ellery Queen* television series

This was typical of the clever way in which Ellery Queen caught his readers' interest by involving them in a mystery outside the confines

Donald Cook (left) as Ellery Queen in *The Spanish Cape Mystery* **(Republic, 1935)**

of the book. Further audience participation was encouraged during the story by interrupting the tale before the final unmasking and challenging the reader to find the solution himself before continuing. Like S. S. Van Dine, Ellery Queen never cheated on his readers during a story and his cases are solvable for those with the time and patience to try.

Publications and Performances

Selected published texts

The Roman Hat Mystery, 1929; *The French Powder Mystery*, 1930; *The Dutch Shoe Mystery*, 1931; *The Egyptian Cross Mystery*, 1932; *The Greek Coffin Mystery*, 1932; *The Siamese Twin Mystery*, 1933; *The American Gun Mystery* (*Death at the Rodeo*), 1933; *The Chinese Orange Mystery*, 1934; *The Spanish Cape Mystery*, 1935; *Calamity Town*, 1942; *Ten Days' Wonder*, 1948; *The King is Dead*, 1952; *And on the Eighth Day*, 1964; *The House of Brass*, 1968. Published in USA by Fredk A. Stokes, New York; and in UK by Victor Gollancz, London.

From 1941 onwards, Ellery Queen stories appeared in *The Ellery Queen Mystery Magazine*, Davis Publications, New York.

On film

The Spanish Cape Mystery. Republic Pictures, 1935. Donald Cook as Ellery Queen.

The Mandarin Mystery. Republic Pictures, 1937. Eddie Quillan as Ellery Queen.

Ellery Queen – Master Detective. Columbia, 1940. Ralph Bellamy as Ellery Queen.

Ellery Queen's Penthouse Mystery. Columbia, 1941. Ralph Bellamy as Ellery Queen.

Television

The Ellery Queen Whodunit (series). MCA/Universal, 1975. Jim Hutton as Ellery Queen. Shown on BBC 1 in 1976.

There is no record of a theatre production featuring Ellery Queen.

Miss Marple

From **The Miss Marple Series** By **Agatha Christie**

Downstairs in the lounge, by the third pillar from the left, there sits an old lady with a sweet, placid spinsterish face, and a mind that has plumbed the depths of human iniquity and taken it as all in the day's work. Her name's Miss Marple. She comes from the village of St. Mary Mead, which is a mile and a half from Gossington, she's a friend of the Bantry's – and where crime is concerned she's the goods, Conway.

Agatha Christie, *The Body in the Library*

Miss Marple is a typical elderly English country lady of the old school. Unmarried, she has lived in the village of St Mary Mead, forever it seems. She appears fragile, has a pink and white complexion, large china blue eyes and is given to wearing lace and home-knitted shawls. She was educated with her sister by a governess, lives in a cottage next to the vicarage and her hobbies are gardening and knitting. She has firm views on morality but can be kind and unexpectedly broad-minded. Some think her a sweet, gentle old thing and others an interfering busybody. Her 'cronies' are other ladies of the parish all of them good souls determined, mostly, on good works but noted for their gossipy prying into village affairs. It is of course true that Miss Marple is fond of bird watching and her binoculars often find more than birds, but Miss Marple is also a student of human nature and this is the root of the extraordinary talent for which she has become famous. Under the delicate old-world image is a brain which is sharp and shrewd. For years she has studied

The late Dame Margaret Rutherford (who bore a remarkable resemblance to Dame Agatha Christie) as Miss Marple in *Murder Most Foul* (MGM, 1963)

village life and through this learnt the intricacies of human nature. Putting her theories to the test, she has often helped to solve minor village mysteries. When a prominent member of the St Mary Mead community is murdered she uses her knowledge of village life (and therefore universal human nature) and successfully leads the police to the true culprit. Soon her methods become well-known and she involves herself in the solving of many murder mysteries. With advancing years her health begins to fail. She suffers increasingly from rheumatism and is obliged to engage old Mr Laycock from the village to tend her beloved garden. Sadly she watches as the fields of St Mary Mead disappear under the building of 'the Development' (the local new estate), but her inimitable curiosity leads her into an inevitable involvement with its inhabitants.

Under medical advice her doting nephew, Raymond West, a rich and successful novelist, engages a Miss Knight to companion her. But Miss Marple's independent spirit refuses to be stifled by the well-meaning Miss Knight who is gently replaced by Cherry and Jim Baker, a cheerful young couple who happily leave the Development to live in with her. Illness does not deter her from sleuthing. When Raymond sends her on a trip to the Caribbean after a bout of pneumonia she still manages to involve herself in, and solve, a murder. Even while acknowledging that her life is nearing its end she cannot break the habit of crime hunting. She is the classic lady of sleuthing.

Miss Marple was the second of Agatha Christie's two most popular and long-running sleuths. The first was Hercule Poirot and of the two Miss Marple was Mrs Christie's undoubted favourite. As time, and scores of books, passed her fondness for Miss Marple grew as did her dislike of poor M. Poirot (qv) who was gradually neglected, leaving her time to concentrate on the lavender and lace of her astute lady sleuth.

All the Christie books reflect the upper-middle-class life in which she herself grew up, and there is a strong feeling of her self-identification with Miss Marple. By all accounts Mrs Christie was a gentlewoman who regretted the passing of the age of gentility. Her early books are pure escapism. They are complex brain-teasers set in a background full of large comfortable houses with French windows opening on to lawns where summer tea is served; or in cosy drawing-rooms, firelit and curtained against the cold outside. The lower orders appear only as servants and there is no poverty unless it is genteel. Crime stems from the inevitable quirks of human nature in beings far removed from the troubled social times of the twenties and thirties. It is no wonder that Mrs Christie's books were as popular as Hollywood in the dark days of the depression.

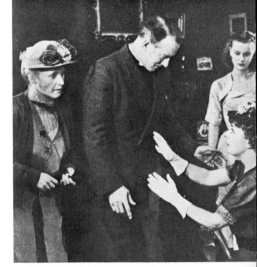

Barbara Mullen (left), the original stage Miss Marple, in *Murder at the Vicarage* at the Playhouse Theatre, London, 1949

Yet Miss Marple and Mrs Christie did not remain in past decades. Within the confines of her own social situation Mrs Christie followed the trends of modern living. In *Nemesis*, one of her later Miss Marple books published in 1970, the council estate moves into St Mary Mead, now rapidly becoming a built-up area, and there is a shortage of servants.

Although her invention and ingenuity never falter, there is a mellow air about *Nemesis* – perhaps Agatha Christie acknowledging the final passing of the old order?

Agatha Christie was born in September 1890 at Torquay. Her American father, Frederick Alvah Miller, was 'a gentleman of substance' who had no need to work for his living. She received no formal education but gleaned what she could from books, and she was greatly encouraged by her widowed mother and her neighbour Eden

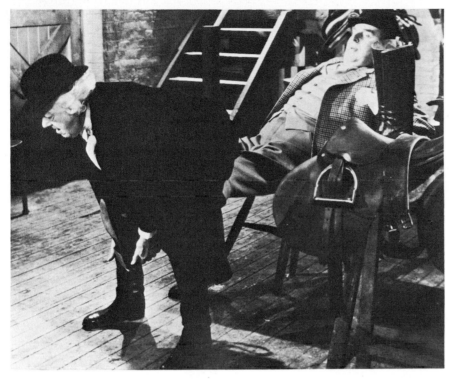

Margaret Rutherford and Robert Morley in *Murder at the Gallop* (MGM, 1962)

Philpotts. After abandoning ideas for a musical career, she began to write poems which were published and novels which were not. She married Archibald Christie in 1914 and began to write detective novels while she was a voluntary war worker (when she also qualified as a dispenser and gained a knowledge of poisons). In 1926 her marriage broke up. She disappeared from Surrey, where she had gone to live, and was discovered three weeks later in Harrogate suffering from amnesia. In 1930 she married the archaeologist Max Mallowan (later Sir Max). After the death of Dorothy L. Sayers in 1957, she became president of the Detection Club. She was created CBE in 1956 and DBE in 1971. She died in 1976.

Publications and Performances

Published texts

Murder at the Vicarage, 1930*; *The 13 Problems* (short stories) (title in USA *The Tuesday Club Murders*), 1932; *The Body in the Library*, 1942*; *The Moving Finger*, 1943*; *A Murder Is Announced*, 1950*; *They Do It with Mirrors* (title in USA *Murder with Mirrors*), 1952; *A Pocket Full of Rye*, 1953*; *4.50 from Paddington* (title in USA *What Mrs Macgillicuddy Saw*), 1957; *The Adventure of the Christmas Pudding* (Miss Marple and Hercule Poirot Short Stories), 1960*; *The Mirror Cracked from Side to Side*, 1962; *A Caribbean Mystery*, 1964*; *At Bertram's Hotel*, 1965*; *Nemesis*, 1971. Published in UK by Wm Collins, London; and in USA by Dodd, Mead, New York. *Sleeping Murder*, 1976; Wm Collins, London.

On film

Murder She Said (*The 4.50 from Paddington*), 1961; *Murder at the Gallop* (*After the Funeral*), 1962; *Murder Most Foul* (*Mrs McGinty's Dead*), 1963; *Murder Ahoy*, 1964. All MGM productions. Margaret Rutherford as Miss Marple.

In the theatre

Murder at the Vicarage. Dramatization of Agatha Christie's novel by Moie Charles and Barbara Toy. Playhouse Theatre, London, 1949. Barbara Mullen as Miss Marple.

Murder at the Vicarage. Revival. Savoy Theatre, London, July 1975. Barbara Mullen as Miss Marple. In March 1976 the part of Miss Marple was taken over by Avril Angers who transferred with the production to the Fortune Theatre, London, in July 1976.

* Published in Fontana paperbacks, Wm Collins, London.

Sam Spade

From **The Maltese Falcon** By **Dashiell Hammett**

Samuel Spade's jaw was long and bony, his chin a jutting V under the more flexible V of his mouth. His nostrils curved back to make another smaller V. His yellow-grey eyes were horizontal. The V motif was picked up again by thickish brows rising outward from twin creases above a hooked nose, and his pale brown hair grew down – from high flat temples – in a point on his forehead. He looked rather pleasantly like a blond satan.

Dashiell Hammett, *The Maltese Falcon*

Samuel Spade, private detective, has nobody on his side except himself and Effie Perine, his secretary. He is a wary acquaintance of both law breakers and law makers and no one is his confidant. A tough loner who rarely wastes time with words, in a crisis his face becomes a wooden mask which would do justice to the most inscrutable of poker players.

After working for a big detective agency in Seattle, he set up in partnership with Miles Archer. He and Archer are purely business partners between whom no love is lost – Archer's wife is Spade's mistress.

Warner Brothers' famous 1941 production of *The Maltese Falcon* with (left to right) Humphrey Bogart (Sam Spade), Peter Lorre, Mary Astor and Sidney Greenstreet

Spade's bachelor apartment consists of a partitioned off 'breakfast nook' in which he cooks, quite capably, for himself and a bedroom which becomes a sitting-room when he has put up the wall-bed. His alarm clock sits on a copy of Duke's *Celebrated Criminal Cases of America*. He smokes Bill Durham tobacco in cigarettes which he rolls himself.

A girl involved in the theft of the Maltese Falcon, a priceless ornament of gold and gems dating back to the Crusades, comes to Sam Spade for help. Through Spade and Archer's involvement with the case, Miles Archer is shot (after which Spade's first action is to

Ricardo Cortez (centre) as Sam Spade in
The Maltese Falcon **(Warner Bros, 1931)**

Ricardo Cortez as Sam Spade with Bebe Daniels in *The Maltese Falcon* **(Warner Bros, 1931)**

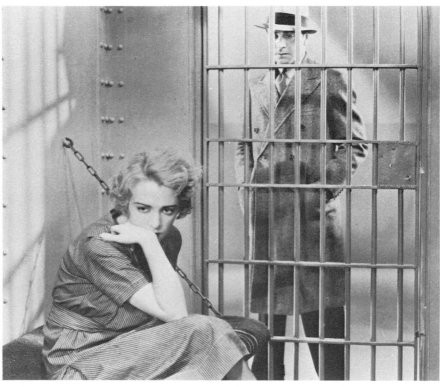

change the name on the office door from 'Spade and Archer' to 'Samuel Spade', and his first resolution is to disentangle himself from Iva Archer, who now expects to marry him).

Spade tackles the trouble with his customary hostile cynicism, suspecting everyone, sparing no one and surprised by nothing. From the gang of villains the girl who first brought him to the case is left to hang for murder. Spade has taken her to bed and realizes he is in love with her. His motive in *The Maltese Falcon* for sending her to the gallows is purely professional:

> When a man's partner is killed he's supposed to do something about it. He was your partner and you're supposed to do something about it. Then it happens we were in the detective business. Well, when one of your organization gets killed it's bad business to let the killer get away with it. It's bad all around – bad for that one organization, bad for every detective everywhere. Third, I'm a detective and expecting me to run criminals down and then let them go free is like asking a dog to catch a rabbit and let it go. It can be done, all right, and sometimes it is done, but it's not the natural thing.

He is left with the unwelcome attentions of Iva Archer. Even Effie Perine, shocked by his betrayal of the girl, has withdrawn her loyalty from him. But he still has his own brand of integrity.

Much of the true grit in crime fiction began to appear during the thirties and this was due in the main to Dashiell Hammett whose cynicism drew the hard line of reality around the soft edges of make-believe. Hammett was an ex-detective (see the entry on Nick Charles) and this added authenticity to the loud ring of disillusionment that echoed through his novels. Although Sam Spade only appeared in one novel (as did most of Hammett's characters, for his book output was very small) he is regarded as the classic of his kind, anticipating Raymond Chandler's Philip Marlowe by eight years. Humphrey Bogart portrayed both Sam Spade and Philip Marlowe on the screen at a time when the cinema was an important medium; and while there was some controversy as to his correct casting as Marlowe, there can be little doubt that his Sam Spade was well-nigh perfect. Thus Bogart probably helped Spade on his way to immortality. But this is a sidetrack, Sam Spade is the property of Dashiell Hammett and the credit must lie with him.

Publications and Performances

Published texts

The Maltese Falcon. New York: A. A. Knopf, 1929; London: Cassell, 1931; New York: Grossett & Dunlap, 1931; Penguin paperback, Penguin, 1935.

The Complete Dashiell Hammett. (Containing 'The Thin Man', 'The Glass Key', 'The Maltese Falcon', 'Dain Curse', 'Red Harvest'). New York: A. A. Knopf, 1942.

The Adventures of Sam Spade and other Stories. Intro Ellery Queen, Tower Books, Cleveland: World Publishing, 1945.

On film

The Maltese Falcon. Warner Bros, 1931. Ricardo Cortez as Sam Spade.

Satan Was a Lady. First National, 1936. Warren William as Ted Shane.

The Maltese Falcon. Warner Bros, 1941. Humphrey Bogart as Sam Spade.

There is no record of a theatre production featuring Sam Spade.

72

The Saint (Simon Templar)

From **The Book Series** By **Leslie Charteris**

Respectability was a disease that could never have attacked a man with a smile in which there was so much unconquerable devilment, it couldn't have found a foothold anywhere in any one of the seventy-four inches of slimly muscular length that separated his crisp black hair from the soles of his polished shoes. And with that smile laughing its irresistible way into her eyes, Patricia felt again as fresh and ageless as if she were only meeting it then for the first time, the gay disreputable magic of that incomparable buccaneer whom the newspapers had christened the Robin Hood of modern crime, and whom the police and the underworld alike had called by many worse names.

Leslie Charteris, *The Ace of Knaves*

The twentieth-century Robin Hood, Simon Templar, is as elusive as the man himself. Because of his initials he is popularly known as 'the Saint', and his origins have never been revealed to the general public. Records of his exploits start when, at the age of twenty-seven, he is living in a converted pill-box in Baycombe, North Devon, attended by his faithful cockney manservant 'Orace, a World War I sergeant of the Marines who limps from a wound received at Zeebrugge.

Templar's intent is to rob the undeserving and give to the

Illustration for *The Man Who Knew* (*Thriller* magazine, 1934). Motorcycle shootings seemed popular at this time (see *Thriller* illustration for J. G. Reeder, page 60)

As the Saint rushed out of his front door, he was just in time to hear the roar of the motor-cycle engine, the sharp report of a gun, and to see the fugitive crook spin round in the road and collapse.

Louis Hayward (centre) as Simon Templar in *The Saint in New York* (RKO Radio, 1938)

deserving. He himself is the main beneficiary of the loot (and no one can say that he is not deserving after what he goes through to get it), but en route, sticking strictly to his own set of outlaw rules, he generally manages to rescue a beautiful girl and eliminate, or at least put behind bars, the undeserving criminal. He is irresistibly handsome, over six foot tall, with black hair and blue eyes, and a tanned muscular body which he keeps at its peak of fitness.

After his spell in Devon, he moves to London and becomes a regular headache for Chief Inspector Claud Teal of Scotland Yard, who admits a grudging admiration for him. Of course Templar does not only operate in Britain and records have been kept of his exploits all over the world, particularly in America. He is not the marrying kind but his girlfriend, Patricia Holm, remains his assistant for some time. They appear to have drifted apart eventually and she is followed by a constant stream of glamorous ladies, all contenders for his elusive affections. A number of helpers appear during his career, one of the long stayers being the pleasantly unintelligent American gun-totter Hoppy Uniatz.

Templar's favourite weapon remains his ivory-handled knife with a six-inch blade which he wears in a sheath strapped to his forearm and hidden under his sleeve; he also carries firearms. Templar lives in Brook Street, Mayfair, is a connoisseur of food and wine and speaks several languages fluently. He is a licensed air pilot and drives a

74

Hirondel and a Furillac.

Guaranteed to strike terror into the heart of the most ruthless villain is the sight of a small card bearing the device of a 'matchstick' man topped by a halo. This is the calling-card of the twentieth-century knight errant who is held in dread and respect by both the criminal and the policeman and whose sobriquet is guaranteed to give them all some bad moments – 'The Saint'.

In the 1890s E. W. Hornung (Conan Doyle's brother-in-law) created a new Robin Hood in the gentleman-crook Raffles. Leslie Charteris's Simon Templar followed in his footsteps as the 1920s version.

In their book *The Saint and Leslie Charteris* William O. G. Lofts and Derek Adley contend that Leslie Charteris based his hero on himself, giving the Saint his own physical characteristics – height, build, hair colour; his own tastes – good living, good food, good wine (Charteris was a columnist for *Gourmet*), good clothes (Savile Row); and his own accomplishments – languages, horse-riding, knife-throwing, flying an aeroplane. Charteris refutes the claim, modestly protesting his incapability to match Templar's 'deeds of derring-do', but admits that he could be the Saint's 'far inferior twin brother'.

The image of a hero who somehow manages to emerge unscathed and fresh from any spot of bother, be it a fight to the death or a small scuffle, has been a perennial favourite since Greek mythology and the Saint is admirable in this respect, as the following extract from *Meet the Tiger* shows:

'Show Mr Templar the door,' said Bittle. 'But how hospitable!' exclaimed the Saint, and then, to the surprise of everyone, he walked coolly across the room and followed the butler into the passage.

The millionaire stood by the table, almost gasping with astonishment at the ease with which he had broken down such an apparently impregnable defence.

'I know these bluffers,' he remarked with ill-concealed relief.

His satisfaction was of very short duration, for the end of his speech coincided with the sounds of a slight scuffle outside and the slamming of a door. While Bittle stared, the Saint walked in again through the window, and his cheery 'Well, well, well!' brought the millionaire's head round with a jerk as the door burst open and the butler returned.

'Nice door,' murmured the Saint. He was breathing a little faster but not a hair of his head was out of place. The pugilistic butler, on the other hand, was not just a little dishevelled, and appeared to have just finished banging his nose on to something hard.

Publications and Performances

Selected published texts

Meet the Tiger. London: Ward Lock, 1928; New York: Doubleday, Doran, 1928.

The Last Hero, 1930; *Knight Templar*, 1930; *Featuring the Saint*, 1931; *The Holy Terror*, 1932; *The Brighter Buccaneer*, 1933; *The Misfortunes of Mr Teal*, 1934; *The Saint in New York*, 1935; *The Saint Overboard*, 1937; *Prelude for War*, 1938; *The Happy Highwayman*, 1939; *The Saint in Miami*, 1941; *The Saint Goes West*, 1942; *The Saint Steps In*, 1944; *The Saint Sees It Through*, 1947; *Saint Errant*, 1949; *The Saint in Europe*, 1954; *The Saint on the Spanish Main*, 1956; *Thanks to the Saint*, 1958; *Trust the Saint*, 1962; *Vendetta for the Saint*, 1965; *The Saint on TV*, 1968; *The Saint Returns*, 1969; *Catch the Saint*, 1975; *The Saint and the Hapsburg Diamonds*, 1976. Published in UK by Hodder & Stoughton, London; and in USA by Doubleday, Doran, New York.

The Saint Mystery Magazine, 1953–67.

Cartoon Strip, 1945–55. In *New York Herald Tribune*, *Evening Standard* (London), *Manchester Evening News*.

On film

The Saint in New York. RKO Radio, 1938. Louis Hayward as the Saint.

The Saint Strikes Back (based on *She Was a Lady*), 1938; *The Saint in London* (based on *Million Pound Day*), 1939; *The Saint's Double Trouble*, 1939; *The Saint Takes Over*, 1940; *The Saint in Palm Springs*, 1940. All RKO Radio productions. George Sanders as the Saint.

The Saint's Vacation, 1940; *The Saint Meets the Tiger*, 1941. Both RKO Radio productions. Hugh Sinclair as the Saint.

The Saint's Return (title in USA *Girl Friday*). Exclusive Films, 1953. Louis Hayward as the Saint.

Le Saint Mène la Danse (based on *The Saint in Palm Springs*). Films Du Cyclope (Paris), 1960. Felix Marten as the Saint.

Le Saint Prend L'Affut (*The Saint Lies in Wait*). Intermondia/TC Productions, 1966. Jean Marais as the Saint.

Television

The Saint (series). Associated Television, 1962–8. Roger Moore as the Saint.

There is no record of a theatre production featuring the Saint.

Cover for a 1934 edition of *The Thriller* featuring a Simon Templar story. Note the Saint symbol in bottom right hand corner

Dick Tracy

From **The Comic-strip Series** By **Chester Gould**

Dick Tracy is an American cop of the violently tough variety. His hook nose and square jaw immediately suggest a prize fighter which, in many ways, describes Tracy perfectly. He is willing to fight to the death for the cause he represents – the elimination of the criminal element in society. This does not make him a gun-toting moron. American cops carry firearms and Tracy is willing and able to use them, but he is equally handy with a microscope, has a fully equipped laboratory and can come up with deductions of a Holmesian quality.

His first publicly known coup is the apprehension of an hotel thief and the 'busting' of a big criminal gang. Although his background is something of an enigma, his second recorded escapade involves his private life. He visits his sweetheart (Tess Trueheart) with the intention of asking her father for her hand in marriage. In the midst of this pleasantly old-fashioned ritual the house is invaded by gangsters who murder the old man when he refuses to hand over his money and later hold Tess to ransom. At this point Tracy is promoted to a member of the plain-clothes squad. In this new role he is able to infiltrate the gang, eventually round them up and rescue Tess. It is eighteen years, however, before the couple are married and produce their daughter Bonnie Braids. In the course of his profession (for Tracy is a professional through and through) he has tangled with villains various. Junky Doolb, Professor M. Emirc, Frank Rellik, Frankie Redrum and John Naem reveal their style of villainy when their names are read backwards. Along with Flattop, Pruneface, Miss Egghead, Mole and so on they have eventually succumbed to

Ralph Byrd as Dick Tracy in *Dick Tracy Returns* (Republic, 1938)

77

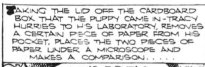

Dick Tracy in a mild mood with a dog and a young assistant

Tracy's uncompromising methods – although he bears the scars of their resistance, having survived shootings, beatings and blowings-up.

A true policeman must be unconquerably resilient and Tracy is certainly that. When his house is burned down in 1970 he is temporarily blinded. But the consternation of his colleagues is unnecessary. Tracy simply puts his deductive powers to greater use and the results are the same.

During his long career he acquires quite a range of gadgetry and even becomes one of the first astrosleuths fighting interplanetary crime.

Dick Tracy was created by Chester Gould in 1931 as a protest against the unlimited and bloody gangsterism, seemingly unchecked by the police, which pervaded the USA during the years of the depression. Tracy was depicted as the hard-line cop crusading against organized crime and sometimes local government, whose laxity encouraged and even condoned criminal activities. Although Gould's artwork is flat and two dimensional (particularly when compared with that of Alex Raymond, creator of Rip Kirby), the violence which he depicted was realistic enough to get the comic strip banned from several newspapers. Dick Tracy was innovatory not only in the comic-strip world but also in the world of fictional sleuths, where readers had met unromanticized violence in the private detective (Sam Spade) but not as yet in an official policeman. Tracy was blazing the trail for countless television series to be churned out later in the century.

The American public took Tracy to their hearts. He proved one of the longest-running serials ever and has spanned the eras of earthbound and science-fiction crime. He appeared in the English *Daily Express* during the early post-war years and in 1960 he was depicted by the pop artist Andy Warhol.

Publications and Performances

Published texts

First appeared in cartoon strip on two succeeding Sundays, 4 October and 11 October 1931 in *Detroit Mirror*; weekday strip *New York News* commencing 12 October 1931, Sunday strip *New York News* commencing 13 December 1931; subsequently nationwide and worldwide syndication. *Chicago Tribune* (New York Syndicate); *Super Comics* (Dell magazines).

On film

Dick Tracy (serial). Republic, 1937. Ralph Byrd as Dick Tracy.

Dick Tracy Returns (serial). Republic, 1938. Ralph Byrd as Dick Tracy.

Dick Tracy's G-Men (serial). Republic, 1939. Ralph Byrd as Dick Tracy.

Dick Tracy versus Crime Inc (serial). Republic, 1941. Ralph Byrd as Dick Tracy.

Dick Tracy. RKO Radio, 1945. Morgan Conway as Dick Tracy.

Dick Tracy versus Cueball. RKO, 1946. Morgan Conway as Dick Tracy.

Dick Tracy's Amazing Adventure (alternative title *Dick Tracy Meets Gruesome*). RKO, 1947. Ralph Byrd as Dick Tracy.

Mark of the Claw (alternative title *Dick Tracy's Dilemma*). RKO, 1947. Ralph Byrd as Dick Tracy.

Dick Tracy versus the Phantom Empire (serial). Republic, 1953. Ralph Byrd as Dick Tracy.

Television

Dick Tracy (series). ABC Television, 1951–2. Ralph Byrd as Dick Tracy.

There is no record of Dick Tracy having appeared in a stage production.

Nick Charles

From **The Thin Man** By **Dashiell Hammett**

Nora could not sleep that night. She read Chaliapin's memoirs until I began to doze and then woke me up by saying: 'Are you asleep?'

I said I was.

She lit a cigarette for me, one for herself. 'Don't you ever think you'd like to go back to detecting once in a while just for the fun of it? You know, when something special comes up, like the Lindb—'

'Darling,' I said, 'my guess is that Wynant killed her, and police'll catch him without my help. Anyway it's nothing in my life.'

'I didn't mean just that, but—'

'But besides I haven't the time: I'm too busy trying to see that you don't lose any of the money I married you for.' I kissed her. 'Don't you think maybe a drink would help you to sleep?'

'No thanks.'

'Maybe it would if I took one.' When I brought my Scotch and soda back to bed, she was frowning into space.

Dashiell Hammett, *The Thin Man*

William Powell (arm outstretched) as Nick Charles in *Another Thin Man* **(MGM, 1939)**

Nick Charles's father was a Greek called Charalambides whose name was unceremoniously shortened to Charles by 'the mug that put him through Ellis Island' when he came over to the USA. After serving in the war, Nick became an ace detective with the Trans-American Detective Agency. A year after he married Nora her father died leaving her a lumber mill, a narrow-gauge railroad and a fortune. Needing no second bidding, Nick retired from sleuthing and the couple settled in San Francisco with their Schnauzer bitch, Asta. Nick spends some hours keeping Nora's financial affairs flourishing with his customary efficiency and the rest of their time is given to parties, first nights, lunches, cocktail parties etc. They seem to live mostly in an alcoholic daze, although Nick is probably more addicted than Nora and even incapable of swallowing breakfast without a couple of early morning drinks (although not that early, he normally rises around midday). Prohibition does not seem to worry them unduly, and if they can't find a speakeasy there is enough liquor waiting for them at home. Both are independent spirits who blend well with their lifestyle which, since they live in the times of the depression, bears comparison with that of Louis XIV and Marie Antoinette just before the French Revolution.

It is their habit to spend Christmas away from home to escape Nora's relatives. One particular Christmas spent in New York proves less tedious than usual when Nora persuades Nick to come (unwillingly) out of retirement and work on a murder case involving some old friends. He solves the crime, preserving his casual self-confidence until the end. In *The Thin Man*, Nora wonders what becomes of people left over after murders, and gets the reply: 'Nothing new. They'll go on being Mimi and Dorothy and Gilbert just as you and I will go on being us and the Quinns will go on being the Quinns. Murder doesn't round out anybody's life except the murdered's and sometimes murderer's.'

William Powell as Nick Charles with Sam Levene, Myrna Loy and James Stewart in *The Thin Man* (MGM, 1934)

The Thin Man was the last of Dashiell Hammett's five full-length novels and, although commercially successful, it has been criticized as lacking the abrasive quality of his earlier work. Indeed, the plush setting of *The Thin Man* is a long way from the harsh disillusionment of Sam Spade's world, but it is still part of Hammett's determined exposition of vice and corruption in America during the depressed thirties.

Hammett worked as a detective for the Pinkerton Agency for eight years. He served in both World Wars, as a sergeant with a Motor Ambulance Corps in the first and as a private overseas in the second. He was an active supporter of left-wing politics. In 1951 he was trustee of the Civil Rights Congress which supplied bail for a group of communists during the McCarthy trials. When four of the group jumped bail, Hammett was subpoenaed for questioning and served a six months jail sentence for contempt of court after refusing to name the source of the bail fund or produce the books of the organization. In 1953 300 copies of his book were found on the shelves of overseas libraries run by the Department of State and suspected of carrying pro-communist literature. Testifying before an investigating Senate subcommittee he refused to say whether or not he was a communist. He upheld that it was 'Impossible to write anything without taking some sort of stand on social issues'. *The Thin Man* gives an ironic picture of wealth and privilege in America during the days of the depression. Hammett never overstated a situation. He allowed it to speak for itself.

Publications and Performances

Published texts

The Thin Man. New York: A. A. Knopf, 1934; London: Arthur Barker, 1934; New York: Grosset and Dunlap, 1935; London: John Lane, 1935; Penguin paperback, 1935.

The Complete Dashiell Hammett (omnibus edition containing 'The Thin Man', 'The Glass Key', 'The Maltese Falcon', 'The Dain Curse' and 'Red Harvest'). New York: A. A. Knopf, 1942.

The Dashiell Hammett Omnibus (omnibus edition containing 'The Thin Man', 'Red Harvest', 'Dead Yellow Woman', 'The Dain Curse', 'Golden Horseshoe', 'The Maltese Falcon', 'Who Killed Bob Teal?', 'The House Dick' and 'The Glass Key'). London: Cassell, 1950.

On film

The Thin Man, 1934; *After the Thin Man*, 1936; *Another Thin Man*, 1939; *Shadow of the Thin Man*, 1941; *The Thin Man Goes Home*, 1944; *Song of the Thin Man*, 1947. All MGM productions. William Powell as Nick Charles.

Television

The Thin Man (series). NBC Television. Peter Lawford as Nick Charles.

There is no record of Nick Charles having appeared in a stage production.

Nick Charles (William Powell) with Ed Brophy, Myrna Loy and Asta in *The Thin Man* (MGM, 1934)

Inspector Maigret

From **The Maigret Book Series** By **Georges Simenon**

Not that he resembled the policeman dear to caricaturists. He had neither moustache nor heavy boots. His suit was of quite good material and cut; he shaved every morning and had well-kept hands.

But his frame was plebeian – huge and bony. Strong muscles swelled beneath his jacket and soon took the crease out of even a new pair of trousers.

He had a characteristic stance too, which even many of his own colleagues found annoying.

It expressed something more than self-confidence, and yet it was not conceit. He would arrive, massively, on the scene, and from that moment it seemed that everything must shatter against his rock-like form, no matter whether he was moving or standing still with feet planted slightly apart.

His pipe was clamped between his teeth. He was not going to remove it just because he was in the Majestic.

Perhaps, indeed, this vulgar, self-confident manner was assumed deliberately.

Georges Simenon, *Maigret and the Enigmatic Lett*

From a poster for *Maigret and the Lady*. Strand Theatre, London, 1965

Jean Gabin as Maigret in *Maigret Tend un Piège* (Intermondia, 1957)

When he was very young, Jules Maigret had wanted to become, in some vague capacity, 'a repairer of destinies', a cross between priest and doctor, whose talent for putting himself inside other people's minds would help to guide their fortunes. The son of a bailiff to a large château, he began to study medicine but left the course uncompleted. Instead he joined the police force. After signing on at the Quai des Orfèvres he went through the humble routine jobs, beat pounding, station patrolman, store detective. After three years he was appointed secretary at the Saint-Georges District Police Station. It was at this point, when he was twenty-six years old, that he married. Enthusiastic and ambitious he conscientiously studied the niceties of his profession through official booklets, and when a case fell accidentally into his lap he set out determinedly to solve it. Because the case involved a rich and influential family he suffered the humiliation of seeing the dénouement of his case taken over by the Quai des Orfèvres. However, his results were good enough to win him his first promotion. A long and successful career has followed, backed always by the loyalty of the long-suffering Madame Maigret. He becomes Chief Inspector of the Flying Squad then Superintendent and is now Chief Superintendent. His methods are those of a born policeman, thorough and stoic. He will himself carry out the menial tasks usually assigned to a junior if he feels it important to the case. But he also has a flair, a certain intuitive insight which raises him above the normal policeman, as may be seen in *Maigret and the Enigmatic Lett*:

> Every criminal, every gangster, is a human being. But he is first and foremost a gambler, an adversary; that is how the police are inclined to regard him, and as such they usually try to tackle him . . . but . . . he sought for, waited for, and pounced on the chink. In other words, the moment when the human being showed through the gambler.

As a young detective, Maigret suffered from moments of depression when it needed all his determination to carry on. He has become famous in the force for his pipe-smoking and the hot stoves that he likes to sit near when he's working.

Age, responsibility, and experience have added a slight irascibility to his temperament. The murder of his friend and disciple, Sergeant Torrence, was one of the most affecting experiences of his career. He and Madame Maigret still live in their old apartment in the Boulevard Richard-Lenoir and his office still boasts an old-fashioned stove. Over the years his collection of pipes has grown considerably.

The Maigret novels must surely stand as classics of modern literature. With characteristic economy of style Simenon has presented us with a living breathing policeman and surrounded him with characters who are certain to go on living long after the book has finished with them. In spite of the rare quality of Simenon's work he has been a prolific writer. At the age of sixteen he was a reporter on the *Liège Gazette* and he published his first novel, *Au Pont des Arches*, at the age of seventeen. When he was between twenty and thirty years old he published around 200 novels under sixteen different pseudonyms. After creating Maigret he wrote a novel in the series every month for two years. At the age of thirty-three he abandoned mystery novels until the early forties. *Les Mémoires de Maigret* is an amusing supplement to the Maigret stories. In the context of crime fiction the Maigret books, for example *Maigret and the Enigmatic Lett*, are an interestingly deglamorized study of routine police work:

> 'Just look at that!' a woman at the Majestic had exclaimed before lunch.

83

Well, yes. 'That' was a police officer, trying to prevent a group of big criminals from continuing their exploits, and determined to avenge a colleague who had been murdered in that very hotel!

'That' was a man who did not get his clothes from a London tailor, who had no time to have his hands manicured every morning, and whose wife had been cooking wasted meals for him for the last three days, resigned to knowing nothing of his whereabouts.

'That' was a senior police superintendent, with a salary of 2,200 francs a month who, once he had finished a case and the murderers were behind bars, had to sit down with a sheet of paper in front of him, make out a list of his expenses, attach all the receipts and vouchers, and then argue it out with the cashier!

Publications and Performances

Selected published texts

Introducing Inspector Maigret (alternative title *The Crossroads Murders*). New York: Hurst, 1933.

Inspector Maigret Investigates (alternative title *Strange Case of Peter the Lett*). New York: Hurst, 1933; published in Penguin paperbacks, London, as *Maigret and the Enigmatic Lett*.

The Triumph of Inspector Maigret. New York: Hurst, 1934.

The Patience of Inspector Maigret. London: Routledge & Kegan Paul, 1939.

Maigret Travels South. London: Routledge & Kegan Paul, 1940.

Maigret and Monsieur L'Abbe. London: Routledge & Kegan Paul, 1941.

Maigret and the Burglar's Wife. London: Hamish Hamilton, 1950; New York: Doubleday, Doran, 1956.

Inspector Maigret and the Killers. New York: Doubleday, Doran, 1954.

Inspector Maigret in New York's Underworld. New York: Doubleday, Doran, 1955.

My Friend Maigret (title in USA *The Methods of Maigret*). London: Hamish Hamilton, 1956; New York: Doubleday, Doran, 1957.

Maigret's First Case, 1958; *Maigret and the Reluctant Witness*, 1959; *Maigret Afraid*, 1961; *Maigret in Society*, 1962; *Maigret and the Lazy Burglar*, 1963; *Maigret Loses His Temper*, 1965; *Maigret and the Headless Corpse*, 1967; *Maigret Takes the Waters*, 1969; *Maigret and the Wine Merchant*, 1971; *Maigret and the Killer*, 1972; *Maigret and Monsieur Charles*, 1973. All published by Hamish Hamilton, London.

On film

The Man on the Eiffel Tower. British Lion, 1948. Charles Laughton as Maigret.

Maigret Dirige L'Enquete. Pathé, 1955. Maurice Manson as Maigret.

Maigret Tend un Piège. Intermondia (Paris), 1957. Jean Gabin as Maigret.

Maigret et L'Affaire Saint Fiacre. Intermondia, 1959. Jean Gabin as Maigret.

Maigret Voit Rouge. Les Films Copernic, 1963. Jean Gabin as Maigret.

Maigret à Pigalle. Riganti-Cervi Productions, 1966. Gino Cervi as Maigret.

Maigret Spielt Falsch. Intercontinental, 1966. Rupert Davies as Maigret.

Maigret und Sein Grosster Fall. Intercontinental, 1966. Heinz Rühmann as Maigret.

In the theatre

Maigret and the Lady. Strand Theatre, London, 1965. Rupert Davies as Maigret.

Television

Maigret (series). BBC Television, 1960–3. Rupert Davies as Maigret.

Perry Mason

From The Perry Mason Book Series By Erle Stanley Gardner

Perry Mason gave the impression of bigness; not the bigness of fat, but the bigness of strength. He was broad-shouldered and rugged-faced, and his eyes were steady and patient. Frequently those eyes changed expression, but the face never changed its expression of rugged patience. Yet there was nothing meek about the man. He was a fighter; a fighter who could, perhaps, patiently bide his time for delivering a knock-out blow, but who would, when the time came, remorselessly deliver that blow with the force of a mental battering-ram.

Erle Stanley Gardner, *The Case of the Sulky Girl*

Warren William as Perry Mason (centre) in *The Case of the Velvet Claws* (Warner Bros, 1936)

Perry Mason represents the unusual combination of lawyer and detective. This solidly built man is an attorney from first to last – he has the habit of hooking his thumbs through the armholes of his waistcoat and pacing the floor when he is thinking, even when he's not in the courtroom. He rarely takes a vacation although his adoring confidential secretary, Della Street, is constantly trying to persuade him to. The few times that he has gone away to relax have been interrupted by potential clients knocking on his door for help – crime seems to follow him around.

His city office is staffed by Della Street, who is obviously in love with her boss and fiercely protective towards him, and Frank Everly, a young lawyer learning the practical side of his profession in Mason's office. Mason likes to conduct his own investigations before a trial, usually involving himself in the rough and tumble of old-fashioned sleuthing. He employs a private detective, Paul Drake, to help him and the two men have worked together for many years.

Out of court, Perry Mason is a man of action whose keen brain can sift through evidence and come up with the truth. In court his rhetoric and knowledge of the law are an impressive combination. He is respected by the police, although he sometimes works against them in order to prove the innocence of a client. After years in his employment Della Street, in *The Case of the Lucky Legs*, still struggles to understand what goes on behind the impassive mask of his face:

Raymond Burr (right) as Perry Mason with William Talman in the CBS *Perry Mason* television series (1964)

'Chief,' she said, 'why don't you do like the other lawyers do?'

'You mean plant evidence, and suborn perjury?'

'No, I don't mean that. I mean, why don't you sit in your office and wait until the cases come to you? Let the police go out and work up the case, and then you walk into court and try to punch holes in it. Why do you always have to go out on the firing line and get mixed up in the case itself?'

He grinned at her.

'I'm hanged if I know,' he said, 'except that it's the way I'm built. That's all. Lots of times you can keep a jury from convicting a person because they haven't been proven guilty beyond a reasonable doubt. I don't like that kind of a verdict. I like to establish conclusively that a person is innocent. I like to play with facts. I have a mania for jumping into the middle of a situation, trying to size it up ahead of the police, and being the first one to guess what actually happened.'

'And to protect someone who is helpless,' she said.

'Oh, sure!' he said. 'That's part of the game.'

She smiled at him from the door.

'Goodnight,' she said.

Erle Stanley Gardner had studied the law since his youth. He was admitted to the Californian bar at the age of twenty-one and practised for twenty-two years (although not exclusively). He was a powerful heavy-set man, described by his friends as 'made of energy and determination'. One of his many interests was the study of human motivation and psychology. All of which points undeniably to Perry Mason as Gardner's self-portrait. Although his writing may not reach the heights of literary genius, the legal twists and turns of his books have been highly praised by his fellow lawyers. The Perry Mason stories have been written by an expert and will always have a particular appeal for the purist.

Publications and Performances

Selected published texts

The Case of the Sulky Girl. New York: Morrow, 1933; London: Harrap, 1934.

The Case of the Velvet Claws. New York: Morrow, 1933; London: Harrap, 1934.

The Case of the Lucky Legs. New York: Morrow, 1934; London: Harrap, 1934.

The Case of the Curious Bride. New York: Morrow, 1934; London: Harrap, 1934.

The Case of the Sleepwalkers' Niece. New York: Morrow, 1936; London: Cassell, 1938.

The Case of the Stuttering Bishop. New York: Morrow, 1936; London: Cassell, 1936.

The Case of the Lame Canary. New York: Morrow, 1937; London: Cassell, 1939.

The Case of the Shoplifter's Shoe. New York: Morrow, 1938; London: Cassell, 1941.

The Case of the Silent Partner. New York: Morrow, 1940; London: Cassell, 1940.

The Case of the Smoking Chimney. New York: Morrow, 1943; London: Cassell, 1945.

The Case of the Lazy Lover. New York: Morrow, 1947; London: Heinemann, 1954.

The Case of the Dubious Bridegroom. New York: Morrow, 1949; London: Heinemann, 1954.

The Case of the Angry Mourner. New York: Morrow, 1951; London: Heinemann, 1958.

The Case of the Restless Redhead. New York: Morrow, 1954; London: Heinemann, 1960.

The Case of the Nervous Accomplice. New York: Morrow, 1961; London: Heinemann, 1961.

The Case of the Screaming Woman. New York: Morrow, 1957; London: Heinemann, 1963.

The Case of the Footloose Doll. New York: Morrow, 1958; London: Heinemann, 1964.

The Case of the Spurious Spinster. New York: Morrow, 1961; London: Heinemann, 1966.

The Case of the Phantom Fortune. New York: Morrow, 1964.

The Case of the Worried Waitress. New York: Morrow, 1966.

The Case of the Irate Witness. London: Heinemann, 1975.

The Case of the Fenced in Woman. London: Heinemann, 1976.

On film

The Case of the Howling Dog, 1935; *The Case of the Curious Bride*, 1935; *The Case of the Lucky Legs*, 1936; *The Case of the Velvet Claws*, 1936. All Warner Bros productions. Warren William as Perry Mason.

The Case of the Stuttering Bishop. Warner Bros, 1937. Donald Woods as Perry Mason.

Television

Perry Mason (series). CBS Television, 1957–65. Raymond Burr as Perry Mason.

There is no record of any stage production featuring Perry Mason.

The Toff

From **The Toff Series** by **John Creasey**

From Lopez the Killer, whose thin-bladed knife had been the foulest weapon in London until the Toff got him, to the lowest-browed pickpocket, they were afraid of the Toff. If he singled out any one of them for his attentions, the victim felt a clammy sensation about his neck, saw a pair of flinty grey eyes wherever he went, and was in a state of perpetual ferment, afraid that the Toff was waiting for him at the next corner, yet not sure that his lean, powerful figure wasn't behind him, waiting for just the right moment to do his stuff.

John Creasey, *Introducing the Toff*

The Honourable Richard Rollison, educated at Charterhouse and Cambridge, where he gained a cricket blue and a first in classics, is an individualist. He has developed an interest in criminology and holds definite views on its comparative values. Some crime he regards with sympathy, and has saved many small-time crooks from the grasp of Scotland Yard. Others he condemns ferociously – blackmail, robbery with violence, drug-trafficking, white slavery, fraud and confidence tricks. All are marked by the Hon R. R. for vengeance.

A legacy from his grandfather gave him the freedom to indulge his fascination with the criminal world, and a year after leaving Cambridge he embarked on a five-year world tour, travelling in the holds of small tramp steamers and cargo-boats. The adventures he encountered broadened his knowledge of crime and toughened him physically. Many a hardened villain finally met his match in the Toff during those five years. News of his exploits began to infiltrate the criminal world and his reputation preceded his return to London. Within a year he had become an object of fear and hatred to some but of trust and admiration to others. At work on a case he uses what he calls 'psychological terrorism', the other man's fears are his chief weapon. His methods are usually frowned upon by Scotland Yard and although he has often brought a criminal to justice for them, his name is rarely mentioned in official records. His immaculate dress, leisurely self-confidence, boundless wealth and magnanimity towards the small-time villain have earned him the nickname 'the Toff'. To help the legend along he carries visiting-cards with his name, address and club on one side and his trademark (a pencilled drawing of a top hat, a monocle and a swagger cane) on the other. During World War II the Toff served in France and Belgium and was at Dunkirk. He has a flat in Mayfair (25g Gresham Terrace), and a cottage in the New Forest. He often visits his father's Norfolk home where he can enjoy a day's cricket (more a religion than a game to him). In his younger days he drove a Frazer Nash sports car, but now he runs a hand-manufactured grey Bristol. Jolly is the name of his lugubrious 'gentleman's gentleman' who has been with him since the Toff's childhood and retains his old-fashioned methods of service whilst managing to remain remarkably independent. The years have mellowed Rollison. Jolly, when asked, in *The Toff and the Sleepy Cowboy*, for his definition of a toff, declares that he is 'A gentleman of high social standing who exerted himself to great good among the less fortunate members of society.' But in the same book the Hon Richard Rollison privately declares that a toff is 'A man who gets waited on hand and foot and is rich enough to give hand-outs.'

John Bentley (left) as The Toff with Patricia Dainton and Lockwood West in *Hammer the Toff* (Butchers Films, 1952)

John Creasey originally created the Toff in 1933 to 'specific editorial requirements' for the twopenny-weekly *Thriller*. Thus restricted his hero was little more than (to quote Creasey's publishers Hodder and Stoughton) 'a rather heavy-footed Saint'. It was not until the Toff went into book form that Creasey was able to direct the character along his own lines. To quote Hodder and Stoughton again 'It was in this period that the author began continually to use the Toff to show how well the Mayfair man-about-town could get on with the rough diamonds of the East End.' Whether Mr Creasey succeeded or not is a mute point. The Toff certainly instilled a cap-doffing respect in the 'rough diamonds' who, whether or not they 'got on' with the 'man-about-town' knew their places and kept to them. Of course it is not fair to judge the early Toff stories by today's social standards, apart from anything else Britain was on the brink of a war which was to change the old order quite considerably. Much later Creasey was the first crime writer to give Scotland Yard credibility in his excellent down-to-earth Gideon series.

Creasey has written under his own name and many pseudonyms including: Ken Ranger, William K. Reilly, Tex Riley, Norman Deane, Michael Halliday, J. J. Marric, Gordon Ashe, Anthony Morton, Jeremy Yorke and Peter Manton.

Publications and Performances

Selected published texts

Introducing the Toff, 1938; *The Toff Steps Out*, 1939; *The Toff Breaks In*, 1940; *Salute the Toff*, 1941; *The Toff Is Back*, 1942; *Accuse the Toff*, 1943; *Feathers for the Toff*, 1945; *Hammer the Toff*, 1947; *The Toff in Town*, 1948. Published by John Long, London – later Hutchinson.

The Toff on Board, 1949; *Kill the Toff*, 1950; *The Toff Goes Gay*, 1951; *Hunt the Toff*, 1952. Published by Evans Bros, London.

The Toff Down Under, 1953; *The Toff at Butlins*, 1954; *A Six for the Toff*, 1955; *The Toff in New York*, 1956; *The Toff on Fire*, 1957; *The Toff on the Farm*, 1958; *A Rocket for the Toff*, 1960; *The Toff and the Teds*, 1962; *Leave it to the Toff*, 1963; *A Doll for the Toff*, 1964; *The Toff in Wax*, 1966; *Stars for the Toff*, 1968; *Vote for the Toff*, 1971; *The Toff and the TT Triplets*, 1972; *The Toff and the Terrified Taxman*, 1973; *The Toff and the Sleepy Cowboy*, 1974; *The Toff and the Crooked Copper*, 1975. Published by Hodder & Stoughton, London.

On film

Salute the Toff. Butchers Films, 1951. John Bentley as the Toff.

Hammer the Toff. Butchers Films, 1952. John Bentley as the Toff.

There is no record of the Toff having appeared on the stage or in a television series.

1933 cover for *The Thriller* magazine featuring the first Toff story

Illustration for the Toff from *The Thriller* magazine, 1933

The Toff heard thunder roaring in his ears as the gas-filled room whirled round him. Then everything went black and he thudded to the floor. A moment later and Anne, too, dropped into a yawning oblivion.

Nero Wolfe

From **The Nero Wolfe Book Series** By **Rex Stout**

Wolfe looked up again, and his big thick lips pushed out a little, tight together, just a small movement, and back again. How I loved to watch him doing that! That was about the only time I ever got excited, when Wolfe's lips were moving like that. It didn't matter whether it was some little thing like this with Durkin or when he was on the track of something big and dangerous. I knew what was going on, something was happening so fast inside of him and so much ground was being covered, the whole world in a flash, that no one else could ever really understand it even if he had tried his best to explain, which he never did. Sometimes, when he felt patient, he explained to me and it seemed to make sense, but I realised afterwards that that was only because the proof had come and so I could accept it. I said to Saul Panzer once that it was like being with him in a dark room which neither of you has ever seen before, and he describes all of its contents to you, and then when the light is turned on his explanation of how he did it seems sensible because you see everything there before you just as he described it.

Rex Stout, *Fer-De-Lance*

Born in America, Wolfe became a secret agent of the Austrian government during his youth. He fought for America in World War I, after which he returned to the Balkans. Here he adopted a three-year-old orphan girl. He returned to America but he left the child to be brought up by a trustworthy couple in Zagreb. (He heard no more of this child until many years later. He was then a well-established detective in America and she reappeared, persuading him to handle a case in which she herself was involved.)

Since his youth Wolfe has grown into a mountain of a man. So fat that he can hardly move. He sits, like an oversized buddha, in his old brownstone house on West 35th Street which is fitted with specially built furniture to accommodate his nineteen stones. He is attended by his assistant Archie Goodwin (who is also his chronicler), his cook/valet Fritz and Theodore Hortsmann the botanist who tends his beloved orchids. He drinks five to six quarts of beer a day and his passions are orchids and food. His orchids, all 10,000 of them, are kept in the glass plant rooms that occupy the entire roof space. They are watched over by Hortsmann who is more devoted to them than to his own life and even sleeps in a partitioned-off corner of the hothouse. Wolfe, in *The League of Frightened Men*, thinks of the orchids as his concubines, 'insipid, expensive, parasitic and temperamental'. He never sells the blooms but gives them away and has gained a reputation for the achievement of botanic wonders. He spends two hours with his plants every morning and afternoon, and nothing is allowed to alter this ritual. Occasionally Wolfe suffers a 'relapse'. This is liable to happen at any time and can last for days. Even Archie Goodwin can find no good reason for these spells. Wolfe will simply lose interest in the world and either withdraw to bed, where he will live on onion soup and bread, or to the kitchen where he spends his time experimenting with exotic dishes which Fritz must cook for him.

Certainly Wolfe is eccentric, but luckily he is also a well-read and scholarly genius. His finely tuned brain ticks over meticulously in his enormous head. While Archie Goodwin acts as his surrogate in the outside world, Nero Wolfe stays in his office minutely picking over the bare bones of a case, reconstructing and rearranging until a solution becomes clear to him. He is unfailingly mean with money and his work is always carried out on a strictly business basis. Owing to his size he hardly ever leaves his flat and his clients must come to him if they require his services. His fame is such, however, that he is usually kept busy even on these trying terms.

By the time Nero Wolfe appeared in 1934, the novelty of a fictional detective who was an eccentric genius was beginning to wear a little thin. In fact from Dupin on it is probably more interesting to pick out those who were not eccentric geniuses. Nero Wolfe, surrounded by the usual array of esoteric penchants – in his case beer, orchids and cookery – would seem to be stuck in the same old groove, but Rex Stout managed to add one completely fresh idea. A detective who hardly moved! The situation created new possibilities in the saga of detective fiction, for whatever else fictional sleuths may or may not have done they were always extremely mobile. The formula produced Archie Goodwin who, cast in the role of Nero Wolfe's ambassador and Rex Stout's narrator, is able to give an objective view of the detective yet a subjective one of the action – in which he is always well and truly involved.

Rex Stout was born in Noblesville, Indiana, but was brought up in Kansas. His father was elected Superintendent of Schools on a Republican ticket. At thirteen Rex was the state spelling champion, a talent which he always retained. After a varied working life which included the navy, clerking and journalism, Stout started writing mystery stories to counter the effects of 'the economic disillusionment' of the late twenties. His first Nero Wolfe novel was well received by both critics and public. He once said that 'writing one of the three best mystery stories in the world would satisfy my soul as much as anything else I can think of'.

Edward Arnold (left) in *Meet Nero Wolfe* (Columbia, 1936)

Publications and Performances

Selected published texts

Fer-de-Lance. New York: Farrar & Rinehart, 1934; London: Cassell, 1935.

The League of Frightened Men. New York: Farrar & Rinehart, 1935; London: Cassell, 1935.

The Red Box. New York: Farrar & Rinehart, 1937; London: Cassell, 1935.

Over My Dead Body. New York: Farrar & Rinehart, 1940; London: Collins, 1940.

Silent Speaker. New York: Viking Press, 1946; London: Collins, 1947.

The Second Confession. New York: Viking Press, 1948; London: Collins, 1950.

In the Best Families (retitled *Even in the Best Families*). New York: Viking Press, 1950; London: Collins, 1952.

Murder by the Book. New York: Viking Press, 1951; London: Collins, 1952.

Triple Jeopardy. New York: Viking Press, 1952.

Might as Well Be Dead. New York: Viking Press, 1956; London: Collins, 1956.

Too Many Clients. New York: Doubleday, Doran, 1960.

Final Deduction. New York: Viking Press, 1961; London: Collins, 1962.

Trio for Blunt Instruments. New York: Viking Press, 1964.

Death of a Doxy. New York: Viking Press, 1967; London: Collins, 1967.

Death of a Dude. London: Collins, 1970.

On film

Meet Nero Wolfe. Columbia Pictures, 1936. Edward Arnold as Nero Wolfe.

The League of Missing Men. Columbia Pictures, 1937. Walter Connolly as Nero Wolfe.

There is no record of a television series or a stage production featuring Nero Wolfe.

Paul Temple

From **The BBC Radio Series Paul Temple** By **Francis Durbridge**

Paul Temple, educated at Rugby and Oxford, hated maths but came to enjoy rugby football (preferring it to cricket which he also played). While up at Oxford he played for his college although he was never a varsity blue. On coming down from Oxford he became a newspaper reporter on one of the great London dailies. After assignments on everything from gossip columns to sports reports he turned to criminology and also wrote his first play *Dance Little Lady* which was presented at the Ambassadors Theatre in 1929. It closed after seven performances. He started writing thrillers and early in 1930 *Death in the Theatre* appeared. It was a phenomenal success and Paul Temple left Fleet Street. After six years he had become established as a highly successful novelist. Through his books and occasional investigative newspaper articles (often leading to the successful apprehension of a criminal), he also became known as a criminologist and his help was sometimes sought by Scotland Yard – usually at the urging of Press and public, for when it was obvious that a case was becoming too much for Scotland Yard to handle 'Send for Paul Temple' was the national cry. Temple's London home was in a large block of service flats in Golders Green. His country house (Bramley Lodge, just outside Evesham) he had acquired cheaply owing to its poor condition, but he had it successfully restored. It became a favourite subject of artists and photographers, most of whom he welcomed, 'only the surrealists did he refuse'. At the age of forty he married reporter Louise Harvey, who had changed her name to Steve Trent in order to escape the clutches of a villainous gang who had murdered her brother Superintendent Harvey of Scotland Yard. The gang was eventually rounded up by Temple.

Temple is an appreciator of good food and wine and his after-dinner cherry brandy is particularly famous. He once smoked both a pipe, briar and cherry wood, and cigarettes, Virginia and Turkish. The Turkish he had made for him by a Greek who kept a café in Shaftesbury Avenue. Now he just smokes a pipe.

Following her former careers as reporter, authoress, wife and mother, Steve has now become a designer. After their marriage the Temples moved to a flat in Mayfair and now have a house overlooking Chelsea Embankment and a cottage, Random Cottage, at Broadway in the Cotswolds. They also have a wire-haired fox-terrier called Jackson.

The thirties and forties were a golden age for radio. It brought entertainment into millions of homes and opened up new horizons for thousands of people all over the world. For many the fantasy world, accessible by merely turning a knob, became reality, daily serials a part of everyday life, and the disembodied voices of the characters as familiar as intimate friends. In Britain Paul Temple enthralled his audiences by extricating himself and Steve from situations that would have made Houdini shudder. Radio is an ideal medium for thrillers. While it is more immediate than a book it is less restricting than films, television or theatre. The location can change as quickly and as often as the author likes without any extra cost, the actors can be crashed, bashed and smashed about without sustaining a scratch, and the listener is free to dream up whatever appearance he wishes for the characters and settings. For fans of the original radio series, Paul

Temple lost much of his impact when transferred to film and television for, however dynamic the action, personable the actors, or exotic the setting, they can never quite equal the individual images conjured up by each listener.

Publications and Performances

Published texts

Send for Paul Temple, 1939; *Paul Temple and the Front Page Men*, 1940; *News of Paul Temple*, 1944; *Paul Temple Intervenes*, 1944; *Send for Paul Temple Again*, 1948. All published by John Long (now Hutchinson), London.

The Tyler Mystery, 1957; *East of Algiers*, 1959; *Paul Temple and the Harkdale Robbery* and *The Kelby Affair*, 1970. All published by Hodder & Stoughton, London; the last title is available in paperback.

On film

Calling Paul Temple, 1948; *Paul Temple's Triumph*, 1950; *Paul Temple Returns*, 1952. All Butchers Films productions. John Bentley as Paul Temple.

Television

Paul Temple (series). BBC Television, 1971. Francis Matthews as Paul Temple.

Radio

Send for Paul Temple, April–May 1938; *Paul Temple and the Front Page Men*, November–December 1938; *News of Paul Temple*, November–December 1939. All with Hugh Morton as Paul Temple.

Paul Temple Intervenes. November–December 1942. Carl Bernard as Paul Temple.

Send for Paul Temple Again. September–October 1945. Barry Morse as Paul Temple.

BBC Radio serials written by Francis Durbridge and Charles Hatton.

John Bentley (right) as Paul Temple with Alan Wheatley in *Calling Paul Temple* (Butchers Films, 1948)

Slim Callaghan

From **The Slim Callaghan Series** By **Peter Cheyney**

Callaghan was five feet ten inches high; his shoulders were broad, descending to a thin waist and narrow hips. His arms were long; his face was thin with high cheekbones, a decided jaw, ears that lay flat against his head. His eyes were of a peculiar blue, his hair black and unruly, and women liked the shape of his mouth. Looking at him one got an impression of utter ruthlessness and a cynical humour.

Peter Cheyney, *Dangerous Curves*

Rupert Patrick (Slim) Callaghan is a down-at-heel private investigator operating from a fourth-floor office (for which he has difficulty in finding the rent) off Chancery Lane in London. He smokes a hundred cigarettes a day which, not surprisingly, makes him cough badly. Every now and again he resolves to cut down on his smoking but he never does. He is five feet ten inches tall, of slender build and has all the sexual magnetism customary in male 'private eyes' of his period. His secretary, Effie Perkins, red-headed and desirable, suffers unrequited love for him; and since 'hell hath no fury like that of a woman scorned', spends half her young life in a suppressed rage.

Callaghan works his cases from a psychological point of view. To him motivation is more important than any number of clues left lying around and he will even falsify evidence to help prove a point, landing himself in many near scrapes with the law. His contact at Scotland Yard is Detective Inspector George Henry Gringall, quiet yet astute, given to doodling fruit on blotting paper. After some years Callaghan rises in the world. He moves home and office to a luxury suite of furnished rooms in Berkeley Square. He wears silk shirts and expensive suits, exchanges his clapped-out old car for a new Jaguar, and acquires a Canadian assistant, Windermere (Windy) Nikolls. His excesses remain much the same – women and smoking – but with the addition of a growing addiction to rye whisky and a habit of rubbing eau-de-cologne into his hair when, for any reason, he becomes overheated. Effie Perkins quite unaccountably changes her name to Effie Thompson, although she does not appear to have married and still nurses her infatuation for Callaghan. He appears to have dodged the World War II call-up, as he continues his 'private eye' work throughout the London blitz, after making a good profit from three or four 'nice little jobs from the Home Security Department' obtained for him by the newly promoted Chief Detective Inspector Gringall.

During the late thirties an American craze, which was to last for several decades, swept Britain. Anything that carried the faintest aura of Americana was immediately fashionable. The influence was most strongly felt through the media, particularly films and radio. An American accent could mean instant fame for a pop singer or an actor, and many affected a form of American-English which became known as 'transatlantic'. One of the off-shoots of the British American phase was Peter Cheyney's Slim Callaghan. Peter Cheyney had been a journalist and song writer before making his name through crime fiction and must have been in constant contact with the new image. There is nothing particularly endearing about the Callaghan books,

Poster for *Meet Mr Callaghan* at the Garrick Theatre, London, 1952. Slim Callaghan was played by Terence de Marney and the play was directed by his brother, Derrick, who became the screen Callaghan in 1954

"It cracks and pops with excitement. . . . A success"

they were, to say the least, inconsistent, shallow and violent. But Callaghan ritualistically womanized, chain-smoked and wisecracked in the approved 'transatlantic' way and Cheyney became a bestseller in Britain and America.

Slim Callaghan was as typical of his period as Victorian melodrama and 1950s realism were of theirs. Anyway there's no accounting for taste.

Publications and Performances

Published texts

The Urgent Hangman. London: Collins, 1938; Penguin paperback, 1949; New York: Dodd, Mead, 1952.

Dangerous Curves. London: Collins, 1939; Penguin paperback, 1939.

You Can't Keep the Change. London: Collins, 1940; Pan paperback, 1951; New York: Dodd, Mead, 1944.

It Couldn't Matter Less. London: Collins, 1941; Pan paperback, 1963.

Sorry You've Been Troubled. London: Collins, 1942; Pan paperback, 1950.

They Never Say When. London: Collins, 1944; New York: Dodd, Mead, 1945.

Uneasy Terms. London: Collins, 1946; New York: Dodd, Mead, 1947.

On film

Uneasy Terms. British National, 1948. Michael Rennie as Slim Callaghan.

Meet Mr Callaghan (adapted from *The Urgent Hangman*). Eros Films, 1954. Derrick de Marney as Slim Callaghan.

In the theatre

Meet Mr Callaghan (adapted by Gerald Verner from *The Urgent Hangman*). Garrick Theatre, London, 1952. Terence de Marney as Slim Callaghan.

Dangerous Curves (adapted by Gerald Verner). Garrick Theatre, London, 1953. Terence de Marney as Slim Callaghan.

Derrick de Marney (left) as Slim Callaghan in *Meet Mr Callaghan* (Eros Films, 1954)

Philip Marlowe

From **The Philip Marlowe Series** By **Raymond Chandler**

It was about eleven o'clock in the morning, mid October, with the sun not shining and a look of hard wet rain in the clearness of the foothills. I was wearing my powder-blue suit, with dark blue shirt, tie and display handkerchief, black brogues, black wool socks with dark blue clocks on them. I was neat, clean, shaved and sober, and I didn't care who knew it. I was everything the well-dressed private detective ought to be. I was calling on four million dollars.

Raymond Chandler, *The Big Sleep*

Philip Marlowe was born in the small Californian town, Santa Rosa. After a couple of years at college he worked as an investigator for an insurance company and later for the Los Angeles District Attorney. He was fired for insubordination and set up as a private detective in Los Angeles. He is smart, tough and cynical – although sometimes he would prefer not to bother with being any of these things. He drives an Oldsmobile, sometimes smokes a pipe but usually cigarettes, which he lights with a Zippo or matches struck on his thumbnail. He has an apartment in the Hobart Arms, Franklin, near Kenmore, and two small, seedily furnished rooms in the Cahuenga Building for his office. He makes good coffee and drinks it with cream and sugar or black and unsweetened. Weighing in at 190 pounds, and slightly over six feet tall, he accepts the occasional beating-up, given or received by him, as part of the job. He was brought up with guns. He started with an old Derringer single shot and graduated through a lightweight sporting rifle, then a ·303 target rifle and a Luger automatic pistol, to a Colt automatic of various calibres and a Smith & Wesson, but nothing larger than a ·38. He once made a bull at 900 yards with open sights. When working he charges $25 a day plus expenses. To live he needs to stay employed, when employed he is overworked, and there's not much time to live. He has read extensively both the classics and modern literature and, as he admits in *The Big Sleep*, 'can still speak English if there's any demand for it. There's not much in my trade.' His conversation is foreshortened and flip, keeping any tell-tale emotion well below the surface. Women are fascinated and usually try to bed him, which he sometimes allows, although he prefers to stick strictly to business with a female client. His lifestyle changes somewhat when he accepts a marriage proposal from Linda Loring, an ex-girlfriend for whom he has nursed more than a passing affection. But Linda is wealthy while Marlowe is comparatively penniless. After the wedding, which takes

Dick Powell (right) as Philip Marlowe with Mike Mazurki in *Farewell My Lovely* (RKO Radio, 1945)

98

Humphrey Bogart (right) as Philip Marlowe with Paul Webber and Lauren Bacall in *The Big Sleep* (United Artists, 1946)

place in Chandler's last and unfinished story, *The Poodle Springs Story*, he finds that he has exchanged the wearisome struggle for survival to one for independence.

Nine years after the appearance of Dashiell Hammett's innovatory private eye, Sam Spade, came Raymond Chandler's Philip Marlowe. Following the Sam Spade formula of the disillusioned world-weary sleuth, Chandler's character was a masterpiece of understatement and throw-away cynicism, but although his novels were well received, he never quite stepped out of the Hammett shadow and always acknowledged him as the master.

Chandler was born in Illinois in 1888. After his parents were divorced his mother took him to England where he was brought up. He remained an American citizen while she took British nationality. During World War I he served with the Canadian forces and the RAF. He began writing the Marlowe books in his early fifties. Like his character he was a realist and remained unaffected by the attention his books received, as he shows in *Raymond Chandler Speaking*: 'So now there are guys talking about prose and telling me I have a social conscience. P. Marlowe has as much social conscience as a horse. He has a personal conscience which is an entirely different matter.'

Publications and Performances

Published texts

The Big Sleep. New York: A. A. Knopf, 1939; London: Hamish Hamilton, 1939; Penguin paperback no 652, 1948.

Farewell My Lovely. New York: A. A. Knopf, 1940; London: Hamish Hamilton, 1940; Penguin paperback no 701, 1949.

The High Window. New York: A. A. Knopf, 1942; London: Hamish Hamilton, 1943; Penguin paperback no 851, 1951.

Lady in the Lake. New York: A. A. Knopf, 1943; London: Hamish Hamilton, 1944; Penguin paperback no 867, 1952.

Little Sister. Boston: Houghton Mifflin, 1949; London: Hamish Hamilton, 1949; Penguin paperback no 1096, 1955.

The Long Goodbye. Boston: Houghton Mifflin, 1953; London: Hamish Hamilton, 1953; Penguin paperback no 1400, 1959.

Playback. Boston: Houghton Mifflin, 1958; London: Hamish Hamilton, 1958; Penguin paperback no 1608, 1961.

Raymond Chandler Omnibus. New York: A. A. Knopf, 1964; London: Hamish Hamilton, 1953.

The Second Raymond Chandler Omnibus. London: Hamish Hamilton, 1962; New York: A. A. Knopf, 1964.

On film

Farewell My Lovely (title in USA *Murder My Sweet*). RKO/Radio, 1945. Dick Powell as Marlowe.

The Big Sleep. United Artists, 1946. Humphrey Bogart as Marlowe.

The Lady in the Lake. MGM, 1946. Robert Montgomery as Marlowe.

The High Window (title in USA *The Brasher Doubloon*). 20th Century Fox, 1947. George Montgomery as Marlowe.

Marlowe (based on *The Little Sister*). MGM, 1970. James Garner as Marlowe.

The Long Goodbye. United Artists, 1973. Elliott Gould as Marlowe.

Farewell My Lovely. Avco/Embassy, 1975. Robert Mitchum as Marlowe.

There is no record of Philip Marlowe having appeared in a stage production.

Batman

From Detective Comics By Bob Kane

After his parents were robbed and murdered while walking home
from the cinema, young millionaire Bruce Wayne vowed to dedicate
his life to crime fighting. After many years perfecting his physical
strength and scientific skills he took the sobriquet 'Batman' and
assumed a bat disguise – black hood with bat ears and half mask,
singlet with a bat device emblazoned across the chest, tights, trunks,
calf-high boots, elbow-length gloves, bat-wing cloak and a heavy
belt bearing several intricate and ingenious bat gadgets. He enlisted
the help of his youthful ward Dick Grayson who is trained to a peak
of perfection second only to that of Bruce himself. The dynamic duo
operate as Batman and Robin the Boy Wonder.

Dick and Bruce live in 'stately' Wayne Manor in Gotham City
with Bruce's Aunt Harriet and Alfred the butler, the rest of the

**Adam West as Batman. West starred in the
20th Century Fox film series that started a
Batman cult in the late 1960s**

Idealised aggression. From a *Batman*
comic

Wayne Manor staff remain unseen but must exist as Alfred could never keep down the dust by himself. Alfred is the only person living who knows the true identities of Batman and Robin. On a table in the library stands a red telephone, the caped crusaders' hot line to police headquarters. Next to the bat phone is a lever cleverly disguised as a bust of Shakespeare. This opens a secret panel which reveals the two bat poles (similar to those in fire stations) down which the stalwart co-fighters in crime slide (niftily changing into their bat costumes as they go) to reach the bat cave, which is their operations room, hidden under the foundations of Wayne Manor. It is full of technical and scientific equipment of the highest sensitivity known to man. After planning their course of action in the bat cave they leap into their fully equipped batmobile ready to roar off to the aid of Commissioner Gordon and Chief O'Hara at police headquarters and plunge into their next tussle with the enemies of Gotham City and the world.

Bob Kane's Batman first appeared in *Detective Comics* in May 1939 and Batman's own magazine started in April 1940. Over the years he has grown from a strip cartoon character to a major industry which has produced films, television shows, comic books and hundreds of Batman accessories.

Aunt Harriet (who is a sweet old lady but dreadfully unobservant and incurious, for she never seems to question the bewildering and ill-explained comings and goings of Bruce and Dick) was a later addition to the Wayne Manor ménage after several ungracious accusations of a homosexual relationship between Batman and Robin – proof that, like many successful comic heroes, he has outgrown the children's market and become an adult cult figure. Children are still his ardent fans, however. When the first television series was seen in Britain there were several tragic incidents of children jumping from windows in an attempt to 'fly' like Batman. In the 1960s Batman's following was on the decline but the timely appearance of a television series, with a highly stylized script delivered with dead-pan humour by the actors, coincided with a craze for nostalgia and the Batman legend was reborn.

Publications and Performances

Published texts

Batman and Robin first appeared in 1939 in *Detective Comics*, published and distributed by National Periodical Publications, Sparta (Illinois) and New York. Their creators were Bob Kane and Bill Finger. Later they were promoted to their own magazine in April 1940, when the first *Batman* comic appeared.

On film

Batman (serial in 15 episodes). Columbia, 1943. Lewis Willson as Batman.

Batman (serial in 15 episodes). Columbia, 1950. Robert Lowery as Batman.

Television

Batman (series). Greenway Productions/Distributed by 20th Century Fox, 1966–. Adam West as Batman.

There is no record of a theatre production featuring Batman.

Telly Savalas as Lieutenant Theo Kojak the definitive tough, American television cop of the 70s (MCA, 1974)

Richard Rountree (left) as Shaft, the black anti-hero of the 1970s, in *Shaft* (MGM/ Shaft Productions, 1971)

(Right, below) Albert Finney as Eddie Ginley in *Gumshoe* (Columbia, 1971)

Jack Hawkins as Commander Gideon with Robert Raglan in *Gideon's Day* (Columbia, 1957)

GOODBYE TO THE GENTLEMEN

In the 1950s, 60s and early 70s, crime fiction gradually transferred itself to television and the policeman took over from the detective.

It was a period of change in Britain. Youth developed a determined independence in the fifties, and juvenile gang warfare started a new reign of terror. The sixties and early seventies was the era of drugs, free love, Carnaby Street fashions and Soho vice rings. Capital punishment was abolished in 1969 and illegal immigration was a new crime. In the mid-fifties John Creasey gave Scotland Yard a 'father-figure' image with his Commander Gideon and, perhaps as an antidote to permissiveness, tough reliable coppers were the new-found successes of detective fiction. In the sixties, however, the popularity of a sleuth was no longer measured by the sale of his books but by his television ratings.

During this time the obsessive American fight against communism dominated most of its crime fiction, particularly in the early fifties during Senator Joseph McCarthy's notorious 'witch-hunt'. The Korean war was fought during 1950–3. In the 1960s came the assassinations of President John F. Kennedy, Senator Robert Kennedy and Martin Luther King, the Red Indian and black communities fought for civil rights, America reached the moon, there was dissension over the protracted war in Vietnam and barefooted flower-bedecked hippies preached peace and love on behalf of the permissive society. As in Britain, the television cop replaced the literary detective, although the American policeman was rougher, tougher and uglier than the British version and wasted little time on gentlemanly formalities. This brand of sleuth was successfully exported to all parts of the world. Through the medium of television, crime fiction reached a new audience and opened a fresh chapter in its varied history.

Inspector Goole

From **An Inspector Calls** By **J. B. Priestley**

SHEILA: I tell you – whoever that Inspector was, it was anything but a joke. You knew it then. You began to learn something. And now you've stopped. You're ready to go on in the same old way.

BIRLING (*amused*): And you're not, eh?

SHEILA: No, because I remember what he said, and how he looked, and what he made me feel. Fire and blood and anguish. And it frightens me the way you talk, and I can't listen to any more of it.

J. B. Priestley, *An Inspector Calls*

A house in Brumley, an industrial city in the North Midlands. It is 1912. A dinner party is in progress. Round the table are seated Arthur Birling (prosperous manufacturer, magistrate, and ex-mayor of Brumley with expectations of a knighthood), his wife Sybil (prominent member of the Brumley Women's Charity Organization), their son Eric, daughter Sheila and Gerald Croft (son of Birling's friendly business rival, Sir George Croft). They are celebrating the engagement of Sheila and Gerald. The atmosphere, warm, comfortable, self-congratulatory, is broken by the sudden arrival of a stranger, Police Inspector Goole. He is seeking information on a young girl who died in the infirmary two hours previously. She had committed suicide by swallowing disinfectant. All indignantly claim no knowledge of the girl. They are overruled by the inspector who, it seems, is no respecter of ex-mayors or future knights and their families. His strangely penetrating questions (based, he claims, on diaries kept by the girl) reveal how a series of events, seemingly unrelated to each other, led to her desperate plight. Each event has been unwittingly instigated by a different member of the party. At some time each has misused his position of privilege and contributed to the wretchedness which led to the girl's suicide. Birling is revealed as a tyrant, Sheila a spoiled, selfish child, Sybil a bigot, Gerald a liar and Eric a drunk and a thief. The inspector leaves. In an attempt to prove him a fraud Gerald telephones the infirmary. They confirm that no young girl has died that evening. The local police claim no knowledge of an Inspector Goole. The whole affair, it seems, was set up. A few moments later there is a telephone call. A girl has died on her way to the infirmary after swallowing disinfectant. A police inspector is on his way to the Birling house to ask questions.

Alastair Sim (right) as the Inspector (whose name was changed from Goole to Poole for the film) in *An Inspector Calls* with Brian Worth (British Lion, 1953)

Written in 1944 and based on material gleaned from Priestley's youth in Bradford, *An Inspector Calls* is perhaps the first and only portrait we have of a chillingly fourth-dimensional police detective. It is not a ghost story but one of Priestley's time studies. Goole is not an insubstantial shadow but a cold reality eerily placed out of context in time. The play is Priestley's comment on the plight of the underprivileged conveniently ignored by the well-fed middle classes of the early twentieth century and Inspector Goole, as the representative of harsh reality, emerges as possibly the first uncosy, forceful police detective in English fiction.

An Inspector Calls was written in a week during the winter of 1944–5. As there was no theatre available for its production in London, Priestley sent it to Moscow where it was immediately translated and,

104

in the summer of 1945, produced by two companies simultaneously. In October 1946 it opened the London Old Vic season where it was unenthusiastically received by the critics. In his production Basil Dean experimented with a set which was swung around and enlarged, affording a different view of the same room for each act. Subsequently the play was also performed in Paris and New York.

Publications and Performances

Published texts

An Inspector Calls. French's acting edition, London and New York: Samuel French, 1948; also in *Plays of J. B. Priestley*, vol 3. London: Heinemann, 1950.

On film

An Inspector Calls. British/Lion, 1953. Alastair Sim as Inspector Goole.

In the theatre

First performed at the Kamorny Theatre, Moscow, in the summer of 1945; first London performance, New Theatre, October 1946 (in the repertoire of the Old Vic Company). Ralph Richardson as Inspector Goole; first New York performance, Booth Theatre, October 1947. Thomas Mitchell as Inspector Goole; revived at the Mermaid Theatre, London, September 1973. Philip Stone as Inspector Goole.

Rip Kirby

From The Strip-cartoon Series By Alex Raymond

Remington (Rip) Kirby, the intellectual private eye, is shrewd, kindly, well read and a lover of classical music, but also tough and hard-hitting. He is a wizard at chess, no mean golfer and at home on horseback (as demonstrated by his adventures in the Western town, Rimfire). He has travelled widely as an archaeological expert and lecturer. Undeviating honesty is mirrored in his handsome square-jawed features, perfectly balanced by his black-framed spectacles. He smokes a pipe and drinks only in moderation. Women of all ages adore him and the younger ones (usually stunningly glamorous) generally fall in love with him, but however mutual the attraction Kirby has never been known to take advantage of it. He lives in a New York apartment attended by his faithful and efficient butler, Desmond. Balding and deceptively frail looking, Desmond accompanies Rip on all his ventures, an indispensable aid to Kirby's battle against crime. 'Not only are you a tower of strength,' Kirby tells Desmond, 'but a very buttress of butlers.'

Kirby is an ace crime fighter, acute and fearless. His continual successes have made him an object of fear amongst villains. As one cornered baddie bitterly mumbles, 'Kirby, now I know why the guys at the correctional facility voted you the flatfoot they'd most like to see hanged.'

One of the great talents of comic strips, Alex Raymond, creator of Flash Gordon and Jungle Jim, invented Rip Kirby in 1946. Kirby is considered to be one of the best comic-book detectives, both in concept and interpretation, to follow the trail blazed by Chester Gould, creator of Dick Tracy. Unlike many of his contemporaries, Kirby does not rely on gimmicks. He has no magic or supersonic powers, is as honest as the day is long and as handsome and clean-cut as a 1940s Brylcreem advertisement, and there is nothing brash about him. He is an intellectual and, unique among comic-strip detectives, has his very own butler. This was not a safe formula for a successful 1940s comic strip, but Rip Kirby proved an asset for the publishers, King Features, which syndicated it in newspapers all over the United States. It has appeared in Germany and Czechoslovakia (as Rip Korby) and was serialized in England in the *Daily Mail* from 1946 to 1974.

In the early thirties Alex Raymond was working on the Dashiell Hammett strip, 'Secret Agent X-9', from which he graduated to two of his greatest successes, Jungle Jim and Flash Gordon. After serving in World War II he resumed work on these two characters and in 1946 created Rip Kirby. In 1948 he stopped work on Jungle Jim and Flash Gordon, concentrating only on Rip Kirby. In 1965 Raymond was killed in a car crash. His work was taken over with brilliant imitative skill by John Prentice (the join is indiscernible). Alex Raymond's delicate use of light and shade lent an added dimension to his work; the unusual angling in some frames gave a curiously cinematic effect. He was a sad loss to the cartoon world.

ROCKS AND HOT VOLCANIC ASH SPEW FROM THE EXPLODING MOUNTAIN.

DESPERATELY, CREW MEMBERS BATTLE AIRBORNE FIRE.

BEYOND THE VOLCANO'S WRATH, GRATEFUL CREWS BRAVE A VAST OCEAN.

Rip Kirby, 1975

Publications

Among the 364 newspapers that have featured Rip Kirby are:

United States

Advertiser, Honolulu, Hawaii; *The Bulletin*, Providence, RI; *Chicago Today*, Chicago, Ill; *Evening Post*, Charleston, SC; *The Examiner*, San Francisco, Calif; *Free Press*, Detroit, Mich; *Light*, San Antonio, Texas; *News*, Buffalo, NY; *News American*, Baltimore, Md; *News and Observer*, Raleigh, NC; *Plain Dealer*, Cleveland, Ohio; *Post-Intelligencer*, Seattle, Wash; *Register*, New Haven, Conn; *Sentinel*, Orlando, Fla; *Star*, Indianapolis, Ind; *Star-Telegram*, Fort Worth, Texas; *State-Journal*, Topeka, Kan.

Elsewhere

Daily Mail, London, England; *Ekstra Bladet*, Copenhagen, Denmark; *Evening News of India*, Bombay, India; *The Express*, Vienna, Austria; *Herald Tribune*, Paris, France; *Irish Independent*, Dublin, Eire; *Le Matin*, Montreal, Quebec, Canada; *Morning Post*, Hong Kong; *Pan American*, Mexico City, Mexico; *Province*, Vancouver, British Columbia; *Smena*, Bratislava, Czechoslovakia; *Le Soir*, Brussels, Belgium; *The Sun*, NSW, Australia; *The Times*, Manila, Philippine Islands; *Die Transvaaler*, Johannesburg, Transvaal, S Africa; *Verlag Neue Presse*, Frankfurt, W Germany; *Vindicator*, Youngstown, Ohio.

There is no record of any theatre or film production featuring Rip Kirby.

Mike Hammer

From The Mike Hammer Series By Mickey Spillane

I laid my fork down and looked at him. I can make pretty nasty faces when I have to. 'Shortly, maybe just for the hell of it I'll take you apart. You may be a rough apple, but I can make your face look like it's been run through a grinder, and the more I think of the idea the more I like it. The name's Mike Hammer, chum . . . you ought to know it down here. I like to play games with wise guys.'

Mickey Spillane, *My Gun Is Quick*

Mike Hammer earned his Private Investigator's ticket and gun licence as a US soldier in World War II. Violent and uncompromising he works from his New York City office assisted by his beautiful secretary (later girlfriend) Velda, who, after working as a secret agent during the war also holds a PI ticket and gun licence. Hammer and Velda plan to be married (in spite of Hammer's seemingly insatiable sexual appetite which he continues to gratify wherever and whenever possible). He drives an old car with a souped-up engine, lovingly fitted by Henry who is a mechanic and an old friend of his. Hammer lives by his gun, a ·45 Colt Automatic US Army model. In spite of his friendship with Captain Patrick Chambers of the New York Police, Homicide Division, he often falls foul of the law which he tends to take into his own hands dealing out brutal punishment to those who are, as he expressed it in *My Gun Is Quick*, 'the rats that make up the section of humanity that prey on people'.

Ralph Meeker (centre) as Mike Hammer in *Kiss Me Deadly* (United Artists, 1955)

Velda, sent on a seemingly simple mission by Hammer, disappears, and he, blaming himself, withdraws from the world and becomes an alcoholic. After seven years he reappears having heard that Velda is still alive but in danger of her life. Her past in the secret service has caught up with her and she is being pursued by communist agents. Alone, friendless (even Patrick Chambers has deserted him after admitting that he was also in love with Velda and blames Hammer for her fate), suffering from the effects of his alcoholism and stripped of his PI ticket and legal right to carry a gun, Hammer tracks down Velda and reaches her two would-be assassins before they can reach her. He destroys them both in his own inimitable way, in the *Girl Hunters*: 'There had to be some indication that people were left who treat those commie slobs like they liked to treat people', he muses while nailing a beaten-to-pulp comrade to the floor by his hand. 'I threw the hammer down beside him and said, "Better'n handcuffs, buddy", but he didn't get the joke. He was still out.'

It has been said of Mickey Spillane that he reversed the whole formula of the art of crime writing, as always before the detective had been on the side of law and order. This is not true, as devotees of Raffles will immediately testify. It is true, however, that before 1947 crime fiction had not met with a private eye so violently anti almost everything, including the law whose style, compared with his own, was, he felt, somewhat cramped by rules and regulations. As he says in *My Gun Is Quick*: 'Some day, before long, I'm going to have my rod in my mitt and the killer in front of me. I'm going to plunk one right in his gut, and when he's dying on the floor I may kick his teeth out . . . You couldn't do that, you have to follow the book.' The Spillane books are

based on uncompromising violence and sex. Their original impact was so startling that Spillane became a best-seller and remained so for years. Written during the aftermath of a world war Mike Hammer, sadistically vengeful, possibly served as a much-needed fantasy figure for men and women suffering the bitterness of war losses. What else he satisfied in the way of human nature it is perhaps better not to dwell upon.

At its peak the popularity of Mike Hammer coincided with the horrific McCarthy communist witch-hunts in the USA. Whether or not this boosted sales of the Hammer books is obviously debatable, but Mickey Spillane has always been at great pains to advertise his extreme anti-communist views. Mike Hammer expends much energy devising unsubtle tortures for the 'commie slobs' he hunts down. Spillane protests that he writes mystery and adventure stories, not detective novels. He dislikes clues and puzzles. In an interview with *Life* magazine (23 June 1952) he summed up Hammer: 'A killer of killers. He doesn't go around just killing anybody. And if he mashes somebody who turns out not to be the killer it's an honest error.'

Mickey Spillane (Frank Morrison) was born in Brooklyn, New York, in 1918. He served as an instructor in the US Air Force during World War II, and on his return to civilian life worked as a crime reporter. In 1952 he became a Jehovah's Witness.

Publications and Performances

Published texts

I, the Jury. New York: E. P. Dutton, 1947; London: Arthur Barker, 1952.

Vengeance Is Mine. New York: E. P. Dutton, 1950; London: Arthur Barker, 1951.

My Gun Is Quick. New York: E. P. Dutton, 1950; London: Arthur Barker, 1951.

One Lonely Night. New York: E. P. Dutton, 1951; London: Arthur Barker, 1952.

The Big Kill. New York: E. P. Dutton, 1951; London: Arthur Barker, 1952.

Kiss Me Deadly. New York: E. P. Dutton, 1952; London: Arthur Barker, 1953.

The Girl Hunters. New York: E. P. Dutton, 1962; London: Arthur Barker, 1963.

All these titles were reprinted in the UK in 1975 as Corgi paperbacks (Transworld Publishers).

On film

I, the Jury. United Artists, 1953. Biff Elliott as Mike Hammer.

Kiss Me Deadly. United Artists, 1955. Ralph Meeker as Mike Hammer.

My Gun Is Quick. United Artists, 1957. Robert Bray as Mike Hammer.

The Girl Hunters. Anglo/EMI, 1963. Mickey Spillane as Mike Hammer.

Television

Mickey Spillane's Mike Hammer. Series produced by MCA/TV 1957–9. Starring Darren McGavin as Mike Hammer.

There is no record of a Mike Hammer stage production.

Commander Gideon

From **The Gideon Series**
By **J. J. Marric (pseudonym of John Creasey)**

What Gideon did not know was that those who had no need to be wary of him were also aware, by a kind of telepathy, that he was here. And of course he didn't really know what he looked like. He realized that he was big; but so were many men at the Yard. It did not occur to him that none of these others had quite his massive hugeness, or his great breadth of shoulder. He was six feet two, and his fondness for the comfort of loose-fitting clothes made him look even bigger than he was. He walked casually, as if out for a stroll, and with a steady rhythm which, given the right circumstances, held a kind of menace. Walking, Gideon looked as if he knew exactly where he was going, and how he wanted to get there, and that nothing and nobody would be able to put him off his course.

J. J. Marric, *Gideon's Week*

John Gregson (centre) as Gideon in the 1960s ATV series *Gideon's Way*

Commander George Gideon of Scotland Yard is six feet two inches of solid policeman. He can be thought of as God's answer to Scotland Yard's prayer. A massive man with the courage of his own

Old Scotland Yard, Whitehall, the original headquarters of Robert Peel's Metropolitan Police Force founded in 1829

convictions, he believes in sticking to the rule-book. His integrity is unquestionable and heaven help the crooked policeman, for Gideon's wrath is terrible to behold. But he is not just another good detective. Long experience of the London Square Mile has given him a valuable insight into the workings of the human mind. He understands (without actually condoning) the motives of the criminal and is concerned for the welfare of their wives and families. He can be unexpectedly sympathetic when dealing with subordinates. They call him Gee-Gee (his initials, G. G., phonetically) and have a healthy respect, tempered with affection, for him.

Gideon's dedication to the force has found its reward in a successful career. At the surprisingly early age of forty-nine he has reached the rank of Commander of the CID. During one day he may be working on four or five different cases and, true to his own standards, each one is given his individual attention as far as is possible. Most mornings he likes an early stroll round his old beat of London's Square Mile. He is at home in a town, uneasy in the country. At one point the strain of his work threatened his private life, and it seemed that he and his wife, Kate, were on the brink of separation. But the ties of their marriage held and in the end gained an extra strength. They have six children, three boys and three girls.

From the earliest days of detective fiction Scotland Yard faithfully played its allotted supporting role as sidekick to the most brilliant stars of British sleuthing. When Sherlock Holmes first outwitted the sadly inept Inspector Lestrade, Scotland Yard became a convenient and fashionable Aunt Sally for British crime writers. Time and again its officials proved no match for the unique talents of Peter Wimsey (qv), Miss Marple (qv), Paul Temple (qv), the Toff (qv) and many others. Scotland Yard, acknowledged as one of the greatest crime-fighting institutions in the world, appeared to be unaccountably staffed by a collection of imbeciles. In the 1950s, however, things began to look up at Whitehall. British television screened a popular series by Edgar Lustgarten of Scotland Yard cases, and in 1955 John Creasey (ironically enough the creator of the Toff) began writing a series of books centred around Commander Gideon of Scotland Yard. Written under the pseudonym of J. J. Marric, they gave a realistic picture of the daily routine in a highly organized and efficient crime-fighting force. Some years earlier Creasey had already published a series of novels about another Yard man, Inspector West, but the Gideon books proved even better sellers. They were made into a highly popular television series and Scotland Yard came publicly of age.

Publications and Performances

Published texts

Gideon's Day, 1955; *Gideon's Week* (title in USA *Seven Days to Death*), 1956; *Gideon's Night*, 1957; *Gideon's Month*, 1958; *Gideon's Staff*, 1959; *Gideon's Risk*, 1960; *Gideon's Fire*, 1961; *Gideon's March*, 1962; *Gideon's Ride*, 1963; *Gideon's Vote*, 1964; *Gideon's Lot*, 1965; *Gideon's Badge*, 1966; *Gideon's Wrath*, 1967; *Gideon's River*, 1968; *Gideon's Power*, 1969; *Gideon's Sport*, 1970; *Gideon's Art*, 1971; *Gideon's Men*, 1972; *Gideon's Press*, 1973; *Gideon's Fog*, 1974; *Gideon's Buy*, 1975. Published in the UK by Hodder & Stoughton, and in the USA by Harper & Row.

Omnibus editions

Gideon Omnibus (containing 'Gideon's Day', 'Week' and 'Night'), 1964.

Gideon's London (containing 'Gideon's March', 'Wrath', 'River'), 1972.

In 1975 *Gideon's Day, Month, Risk, Fire, March, Lot, Wrath, River, Power, Art, Men* and the omnibus edition of *Gideon's London* were reprinted as Coronet paperbacks (Hodder & Stoughton).

On film

Gideon's Day (retitled *Gideon of Scotland Yard* in USA). Columbia Pictures, 1957. Jack Hawkins as Commander Gideon.

Television

Gideon's Way (series). ATV Television, 1964–5. John Gregson as Commander Gideon.

There is no record of any stage production featuring Gideon.

Jack Hawkins (centre) as Commander Gideon in *Gideon's Day* (Columbia, 1957)

Piet Van der Valk

From The Van Der Valk Series By Nicolas Freeling

The bureaucratic octopus spent plenty of time telling him off, drawing magic circles outside which he might not step, and devising new sets of rules. He broke these, of course – all policemen had to if they were ever to get any work done at all – and wasted a good deal of time in not-getting-caught; already a terrible indictment of his efficiency, that, when he considered the further immense amounts of time consumed in writing reports. So little of what one did made any sense. One lived in a Kafka world: he supposed it helped him a little to look at the castles and the trials, to realize why the examining magistrate behaved in that neurotic way (so like a goose deprived of its partner in the triumph ceremony), but Kafka was not a writer he cared for.

Nicolas Freeling, *Over the High Side*

In 1925, in Pijp, a poor district in Amsterdam, Holland, Piet Van der Valk, the son of an artisan carpenter, was born. A bright child, he was educated at Hogere Burger School (a superior sort of grammar school) with the children of the petty-bourgeois, who jeered at his accent and his street manners. He became a soldier during World War II (when both his parents were killed). In 1943 he fled, via Sweden, to England, where he was kept in an internment camp for several months. Back in Amsterdam after the war he was accepted as a trainee officer of police. He gained several law degrees.

In 1947 he met and married his wife Arlette. The well-educated rebellious daughter of a French landowner, Arlette, a superb cook and natural homemaker, is a source of strength to Piet. Basically a spontaneous emotional woman she occasionally surprises him with her resilience and single-mindedness. He is a clever and conscientious policeman but apt to break the rules of officialdom, preferring to follow his own. Vital to him are the copious and seemingly incomprehensible notes that he makes, and studies avidly, while working on a case. His egotistical lack of respect for 'superior mediocrities' and his indiscretion worked against his otherwise bright chances of early promotion, and the couple lived in poverty in Amsterdam for twenty years. Physically almost awkwardly large, Piet is well read and widely travelled. The natural objective humanity of the man balances a brutish joviality acquired for professional use. Although sexually very aware he has been unfaithful to Arlette only once. The ensuing constraint between them was short-lived.

After a few typically random but nevertheless spectacular successes, Van der Valk has worked his way up the promotion ladder in different divisions of the Amsterdam Police Corps. A bullet wound left him with a permanently 'gammy' leg and he was then transferred to quieter suburban assignments. After twenty-five years, when he is on the brink of retirement and accepting a disappointing end to his career, he is awarded a prestigious post in a government commission set up to co-ordinate European criminal social studies. With this appointment goes the title 'Principal Commissaire', a cramped flat and an equally cramped office in The Hague.

While experimenting unofficially and only half seriously in private detection he accidentally comes in contact with Larry Saint, a fraudulent dealer in art and sex. On his guard against police

113

interference, Saint arranges for the annihilation of the Commissaire and on a rain-soaked third day of March Van der Valk is shot down in the street. Arlette, who throughout her husband's life had remained firmly uninvolved in his police work, successfully hunts down his killer with the help of a circle of friends from Amsterdam.

Piet Van der Valk's epitaph, inscribed on his tombstone near the little cottage in France that he and Arlette bought for their retirement, is a quotation from Horace:

Quam si clientum longa negotia
Dijudicata lite relinqueret.

(As if they were his clients and he had settled
Some lengthy lawsuit for them and was leaving.)

Odes of Horace III, v, 14

The Van der Valk novels can be said to have represented something of a milestone in crime writing, having won praise from crime and non-crime readers alike. Van der Valk has been hailed as the greatest European detective since Maigret and with the expansion of the Common Market he was a timely addition to the annals of crime fiction. Van der Valk was not merely a second Maigret, however. Freeling has too individual a style for any such label. The increasing speed of travel and communications could have made him truly international had not Freeling killed him off before there was time for him to really extend his boundaries.

Nicolas Freeling, who was born in London in 1927 and brought up in France, wrote his tales of the Dutch Police Commissaire while he worked as a professional cook in Europe. After the success of *Love in Amsterdam*, he abandoned cooking but has brought out his own highly successful cookery book.

Publications and Performances

Published texts

Love in Amsterdam. London: Victor Gollancz, 1962; New York: Harper & Row, 1962; Penguin paperback, 1965.

Because of the Cats. London: Victor Gollancz, 1963; New York: Harper & Row, 1964; Penguin paperback, 1965.

Gun before Butter. London: Victor Gollancz, 1963; Penguin paperback, 1965.

Double Barrel. London: Victor Gollancz, 1964; New York: Harper & Row, 1964; Penguin paperback, 1967.

Criminal Conversation. London: Victor Gollancz, 1965; New York: Harper & Row, 1966; Penguin paperback, 1967.

King of the Rainy Country. New York: Harper & Row, 1965; London: Victor Gollancz, 1966; Penguin paperback, 1968.

Tsing-Boum. London: Hamish Hamilton, 1969; New York: Harper & Row, 1969; Penguin paperback, 1971.

Lovely Ladies (retitled *Over the High Side*). New York: Harper & Row, 1971; London: Hamish Hamilton, 1972.

A Long Silence. London: Hamish Hamilton, 1972.

Television

Thames Television series. Starring Barry Foster as Van der Valk.

There is no record of any feature film or stage production relating to this character.

Barry Foster (right) as Van der Valk with Sidney Tafler in the Thames Television series *Van Der Valk*

Inspector Clouseau

From **The Clouseau Film Series** By **Blake Edwards**

Clouseau is a startlingly clumsy French detective who has muddled his way through life leaving chaos in his wake. By seemingly miraculous coincidence none of the havoc caused by Clouseau's uncoordinated incompetent efforts as a working detective have any lasting ill-effects on Clouseau himself. Amazingly he always manages to benefit in the long run. His diligent efforts to track down the notorious jewel thief known as the 'Phantom' result in his own conviction and imprisonment while the real 'Phantom' makes off with Clouseau's beautiful wife, Simone. Even in these dire circumstances Clouseau's luck holds, for as a bold, bad jewel thief he finds himself the object of mass feminine hero-worship.

Unscathed by this adventure he carries on to survive the frustrated wrath of a superior officer who, in the face of Clouseau's blatant misreading of clues and obstinate refusal to accept the guilt of a lady suspected of murder, is driven to attempt his assassination by a few strategically placed bombs. Everyone is blown up except Clouseau, who survives to get the girl – as it happens, she does turn out to be innocent. Thus Inspector Clouseau blunders on. A sure-fire loser who maddeningly always wins.

In an uncaring world moving at breakneck speed, the Clouseau films are an oasis of sanity. For Inspector Clouseau is not just funny, he is also able to make the most dull-witted of us feel instantly superior in intellect and understanding. Not a case has he tackled without our realizing how much more efficiently we could have handled it. The man makes us feel positively intelligent. A rare gift this, unusual in detectives. Can the same be said for Nero Wolfe (qv), Sherlock Holmes (qv) or Rin Tin Tin (qv)? Jacques Clouseau is unique among sleuths.

Peter Sellers as Clouseau in *The Pink Panther*, 1962

The Clouseau films were the brainchild of the American film actor/ producer/director/scriptwriter Blake Edwards. He was born in Tulsa, Oklahoma, in 1922 (his real name is William Blake McEdward). He was educated at Beverly Hills High School. As an actor his first feature-film appearance was in a small role in *Ten Gentlemen from West Point* in 1942. His first feature film as a scriptwriter was *Panhandle* in 1948, which he also produced. He has worked as a radio writer and television director/writer.

Performances
On film
The Pink Panther. United Artists, 1962. Peter Sellers as Inspector Clouseau.

A Shot in the Dark. United Artists, 1964. Peter Sellers as Inspector Clouseau.

Inspector Clouseau. United Artists, 1968. Alan Arkin as Inspector Clouseau.

Return of the Pink Panther. United Artists, 1975. Peter Sellers as Inspector Clouseau.

Television
In 1969 a television cartoon series featuring Inspector Clouseau and the Pink Panther was produced by Warner Brothers. It was originally televised by the NBC and later shown on BBC Television.

There is no record of any Inspector Clouseau stage production, and to date this fictional detective has not been portrayed in a book.

Peter Sellers (right) as Clouseau with
John Le Mesurier in *The Pink Panther*
(United Artists, 1962)

John Shaft

From **The Shaft Series** By **Ernest Tidyman**

His body almost always felt good. He knew its value, from the first beating it survived, from the first club-swinging cop it had outrun through a trash-cluttered alley, from the first concrete chasm it had leaped between Harlem tenements, from the bullets it had survived.

Shaft's face was gentle, open, snuggled against the pillow. It was more round than oval, more flat and concave than sculptured and convex. The eyes and nose seemed to have been cut into it, rather than built upon it. It was almost a Polynesian carved face, cut into stained balsa or some dark wood. The lips were full, but they lay flat against his teeth. A mask, but not a mask. Even in sleep there was life in it. Life and strength. It was framed in a modified Afro haircut, notched with unexpectedly delicate and tightly set ears.

Ernest Tidyman, *Shaft*

Shaft is a black private detective living in Greenwich Village and working from his office in Times Square. Brought up in Harlem by the Welfare Department he can remember only some of his foster mothers, Mrs Iggleston, Mrs Johnson, and Mrs Underwood – 'a nice old bitch' who drank too much but kept him comparatively clean. His childhood, spent evading the police and staying alive in street brawls, has provided him with underworld contacts invaluable in his profession. His friendship with the overworked John Anderozzi, Police Lieutenant of the precinct, is wary but on the whole durable and mutual respect allows their frequent collaboration.

Shaft keeps himself fit, knowing that his life can depend on the quickness of his reflexes. His strong and agile body carries a number of scars to remind him – the bicycle chain which he failed to evade in a Harlem street fight, three bullet wounds in his left thigh and side (a present from the Vietnam war), and various momentoes picked up during the normal course of his work. His clothes are also important to him, he is uncomfortable in a soiled suit. His apartment is usually a mess. He rarely goes there and never has time to tidy up, although he occasionally regrets the unswept floor which barefooted chicks must walk on when they leave his bed. He is ruthless and will not hesitate to kill if threatened. He has lifted a man and thrown him to his death through the (closed) window of his office. Women find him irresistible and he tends to use them with the same speed that other people use paper tissues. Shaft's problem is never how to get them but always how to be rid of them. 'What do you do with them,' he asks, 'when you've done with them?'

When Anderozzi is blown to pieces by a bomb placed in his car, Shaft, intent on avenging the death of his only friend, breaks up a Mafia network and collects a substantial reward on the way. But revenge is empty for it cannot bring Anderozzi back from the grave. Shaft returns to his darkened apartment. In the shadows a gunman waits for his return with the money. Before there is time to switch on a light John Shaft lies dead on the floor.

In the 1950s Ian Fleming created the first anti-superhero, James Bond. Bond was tough, sophisticated, white and a product of the English ruling classes. Hard on his heels came Ernest Tidyman's 1970s anti-

**Richard Rountree as Shaft in *Shaft*
(MGM/Shaft Productions, 1971)**

superhero, John Shaft. Shaft, like Bond, is tough and sophisticated but twenty years has changed the rest of the image. Today's anti-superhero is black and comes from the underprivileged of American society. Bond's assets are a good education and a stiff upper lip. Shaft's a street education and a well-developed sense of self-preservation.

Ernest Tidyman created Shaft in 1970. The first Shaft film, in 1971, earned an Oscar for Isaac Hayes as composer of the best original film score. Tidyman, who wrote the screenplay for *The French Connection* as well as the Shaft films, is also a television and film producer.

Publications and Performances

Published texts

Shaft. New York: Macmillan, 1970 (Cock Robin Mystery Stories); London: Michael Joseph, 1971; New York: Bantam paperback, 1971; London: Corgi paperback, 1972.

Shaft's Big Score. New York: Bantam paperback, 1972; London: Corgi paperback, 1972.

Shaft among the Jews. New York: Dial Press, 1972; London: Weidenfeld & Nicolson, 1973; Corgi paperback, 1973.

Shaft Has a Ball. New York: Bantam paperback, 1973; London: Corgi paperback, 1973.

Shaft's Carnival of Killers. New York and London: Bantam paperback, 1974.

Goodbye Mr Shaft. New York: Dial Press, 1974; London: Weidenfeld & Nicolson, 1974.

The Last Shaft. New York: Bantam paperbacks, 1975; London: Weidenfeld & Nicolson, 1975.

On film

Shaft. MGM/Shaft Productions, 1971. Richard Rountree as Shaft.

Shaft's Big Score. MGM/Shaft Productions, 1972. Richard Rountree as Shaft.

Shaft in Africa. MGM/Shaft Productions, 1973. Richard Rountree as Shaft.

Television

MGM/CBS Television series. Starring Richard Rountree as Shaft. Shown in Great Britain by Granada Television.

There is no record of any stage production featuring Shaft.

Eddie Ginley

From **Gumshoe** By **Neville Smith**

Now the late fifties, that's my time, that's where I'm sticking. That's where I'm stuck, too, with almost everything, clothes, records – movies I'm stuck with in the forties. The mountain of trivia that is enclosed by my skull hails from way back. Anyway, next to my suit is my new tux; I'm still paying for it so it must be new, but I give you odds you'd never think so when I've got it on. I've got some good things in my modest little stash, a wall 'phone in the kitchen for instance, and my bookshelves are crammed with several interesting titles – nearly all the Penguin greenbacks; lots of different books really, a pretty catholic taste that remained when my ugly Catholic religion got the boot. Next to the bookshelves is my record collection and my hi-fi set up; Thorens 150 deck, Nicco amp, and Celestion 15 speakers for the buffs out there. On the little mantelpiece I have, there is a ten by eight of Lauren Bacall, a ten by eight of me in my tux – a Jerome's special photograph ('Look showbiz,' the photographer said) – a framed colour photograph of the 1970 League Champions, my cufflink collection and a birthday card: 'Now you are 31!' A joke one, Ellen sent me that.

Neville Smith, Gumshoe

Eddie Ginley is a Liverpudlian, living on the top floor of a house in Gambier Terrace, the front window of which faces the Anglican Cathedral. He is a graduate of Hull University, ex-Teddy-boy, football fan, avid reader of American detective novels and a member of the dole queue. He works evenings at the Clubmoor and West Derby Social and Working Man's Club (known, owing to its location, as the Broadway), calling Bingo and announcing the acts. Tommy Summers, boss of the Broadway, discovered Eddie entertaining OAPs in a Labour club and employed him, promising him a chance to work in his act. There's more of Archie Rice than Lenny Bruce in Eddie's act, yet Eddie himself is deceptive. Master of the flip-quip he sentimentalizes the past (Humphrey Bogart, Philip Marlowe, Buddy Holly, Elvis Presley) but views the present with a jaundiced anti-Establishment eye. His parents died within a year of each other. Eddie's traumatic attempts to compensate for his brother William's callous disinterest in his dying father and William's marriage to Ellen, who was Eddie's girl, have resulted in Eddie's weekly trips to a psychiatrist. ('I'd gone hypochondriac badly.') He smokes heavily (Lucky Strikes, which he lights with a Zippo lighter), but a disillusioned detachment has kept him off drugs and drink.

On his thirty-first birthday, as a joke present to himself, he places an advertisement in the *Echo*:

> SAM SPADE
> Ginley's the name
> Gumshoe's the game
> Private Investigations
> No Divorce Work
> 051-246-4379

The joke misfires. Eddie is summoned to the Plaza Hotel, suite 105, where he finds a parcel containing £1000, a photo of a girl, and a Smith & Wesson, five-shot, walnut-stacked, police special. Eddie

becomes embroiled in a real-life five-star Humphrey Bogart-type drama which runs the sickening gamut of murder, blackmail and drug rings, motivated by the kidnapping of the daughter of a South African communist. As the tangle is unravelled, William and Ellen are revealed as part of the crooked set-up.

The Gumshoe gag has backfired on Eddie. His brother and Ellen have been arrested. He is involved with the law (Eddie distrusts the police no matter which side he is on), and along the way William has blackmailed him out of his club job. On the record player Elvis urges 'Go Cat Go'.

'Yeah, sure,' I thought. 'But go where, Elvis? Go where?'

As an amateur sleuth, Eddie Ginley demonstrates the dangers of confusing fact with fantasy in the criminal world. Together with sport and show business the private detective has become glamourized beyond all professional recognition. The average factual private investigator makes his living with divorce cases and bad debts – kidnappings and international incidents do not often come his way. But if they should it would be as well for the sleuth in question to be an experienced professional not an enthusiastic amateur. Neville Smith had Eddie Ginley find this out the hard way.

The heroes of authors such as Raymond Chandler and Dashiell Hammett appear to belong in the real world, they are as human as the rest of us, it seems they possess just that little extra in brains or physique which could surely be cultivated by a man of average ability. But on closer scrutiny, a fine outer-coating of glitter dust may just be discerned. This protective layer can only be acquired through the pens of novelists and screen writers or the skill of actors.

Neville Smith, football, film, and Raymond Chandler fan was born into a Liverpudlian working-class family. He became an actor and playwright, writing for radio and television. Following a visit to a film preview he became involved in a discussion with Maurice Hatton and Stephen Frears on Raymond Chandler, during which he declared that he could write a thriller. With the help of Frears and Hatton he produced the film script of *Gumshoe*. He wrote the part of Eddie Ginley for himself, but Albert Finney eventually played the role, Smith appearing as the local gun expert.

Publications and Performances

Published texts

Gumshoe. London: Collins, Fontana paperback, 1971.

On film

Gumshoe. Columbia Pictures, 1971. Albert Finney as Eddie Ginley.

There is no record of any *Gumshoe* stage production.

Albert Finney (right) as Eddie Ginley with George Silver in *Gumshoe* (Columbia, 1971)

Theo Kojak

From **The Television Series** Created by **Abby Mann**

Maybe I do best what I get angry at. I mean, when I was a patrolman, I couldn't really get into rousting winos out of doorways and pouring them into paddy wagons. And I couldn't get off on closing down joke-shop operators who sold Cuban playing cards with the out-of-focus broads trying to smile. Victimless crimes. But people who got killed or hurt or shafted badly – that made me mad, and I did better, put in more time, and made more arrests that held up in court. You've got a lot of rights. But one of them isn't the right to hurt somebody else. *Nobody* has that right.

Victor B. Miller, *Requiem for a Cop*

Telly Savalas as Theo Kojak in *The Chinatown Murders* **(MCA/Universal, 1974)**

Theo Kojak is the son of Greek immigrants who rode steerage to the promised land of America. After fighting his way through police academy ('Of all the schooling I got the only place I learnt anything useful was here'), he runs the gamut of patrol work and beat pounding with the single-minded drive and self-confidence of a good New York cop, until he makes plainclothes status. Now after twenty years in the police force he is Lieutenant Kojak, working out of Manhattan South Detectives from his office in the thirteenth precinct building located between First and Second Avenue.

Immediately superior to Lieutenant Kojak is Captain McNeill. For many years Kojak and McNeill worked together. Maybe it was Kojak's blunt and sometimes unorthodox approach to his work or a tendency to act on his emotions (he can be as sentimental over a friend as he can be repulsed by an enemy) that affected his promotion chances. Whatever the reason it is McNeill who has made captain while Kojak remains a lieutenant. Yet McNeill would be one of the first to acknowledge Kojak as the better detective in the end. Kojak's work is his life. It destroyed his marriage: when the time came to choose between wife and work, the police force won. Now his loyalties belong entirely to the force. He is completely incorruptible – although he may bend the rules if it will help bring a criminal to justice. His compassion is for the kicked-around underdog. Bullying con-men and protection racketeers get short

From Edgar Allan Poe's Chevalier Dupin to the American cop. The badge of a New York police lieutenant

123

shrift from him. There's little doubt about Kojak's qualities of leadership. The men under his jurisdiction know better than to question his decisions, and in return for their loyalty he offers them a fierce protection.

The Manhattan South Detectives cover an area that runs from 61st to the Battery, the East River to the Hudson and crime fighting keeps Kojak occupied most of his days and nights. When he can find time, however, he watches basketball and boxing, plays poker and is a bit of a pool hustler. He is a large man (he has described himself as a carthorse) with a head as innocent of hair as a billiard ball. Hearth and home are not what he is about, although it could be argued that most people need something to hang on to. The Tootsie-Roll Pops that the lieutenant chews on could be his security blanket. On the other hand perhaps he just likes them.

Kojak, the creation of Abby Mann, came to the small screen in the early seventies when the tough, ugly American detective was beginning to become the vogue in television series. Before the coming of the whodunits to television, the Western reigned supreme in America. In Britain viewers had been watching such popular home-grown series as Edgar Lustgarten's *Scotland Yard*, *No Hiding Place* and *Dixon of Dock Green*. In the late fifties the American cop burst on the international television screen with Jack Webb as Sergeant Friday in *Dragnet*. Webb's skilful underplaying and deadpan intoning ('This is the city. I'm a cop. I want the facts, ma'am. Just the facts.') made him a household name overnight. For a while the cowboy and the American detective ran neck and neck in the popularity stakes. *Seventy Seven Sunset Strip* gave way to Raymond Burr as *Perry Mason*, which in turn gave way to Raymond Burr in a wheelchair, as *Ironside*. Britain introduced a new hard-hitting-formula police series *Z Cars* which challenged the homely British-bobby image of *Dixon of Dock Green* but never succeeded in killing it. A British innovation, *The Avengers*, a study in understatement with an underlying hint of sex and a touch of phantasmagoria, broke new ground in the sixties both in Britain and America.

Hawaii Five O heralded the arrival of the American detective boom in the seventies. This series was enhanced by its locale of sun-kissed beaches, waving palms and rolling surf. It also featured Hawaiian actors (some years earlier *I Spy* had co-starred black actor Bill Cosby and white actor Robert Culp with considerable success). The Western finally merged with the whodunit in *McCloud*, with Dennis Weaver playing a hick sheriff posted to New York.

Then came the heavy brigade, *Cannon* (William Conrad), *Columbo* (Peter Falk) and *Kojak* (Telly Savalas). Telly Savalas made a chart-topping record, 'If', which established him as a modern heart-throb and the era of the (seemingly) irresistible 'uglies' had firmly established itself.

Publications and Performances

Published texts

In USA: *Siege*; *Requiem for a Cop*; *The Girl in the River*; *Therapy in Dynamite*; *Death Is Not a Passing Grade*; *A Very Deadly Game*. All New York: Simon & Schuster, Pocket Book paperbacks.

In UK: *Requiem for a Cop*; *The Girl in the River*; *Marked for Murder*. London: W. H. Allen, Star Books paperbacks.

Television

MCA/Universal Series. Starring Telly Savalas as Kojak. Originally shown on CBS Television. Shown in UK on BBC Television.

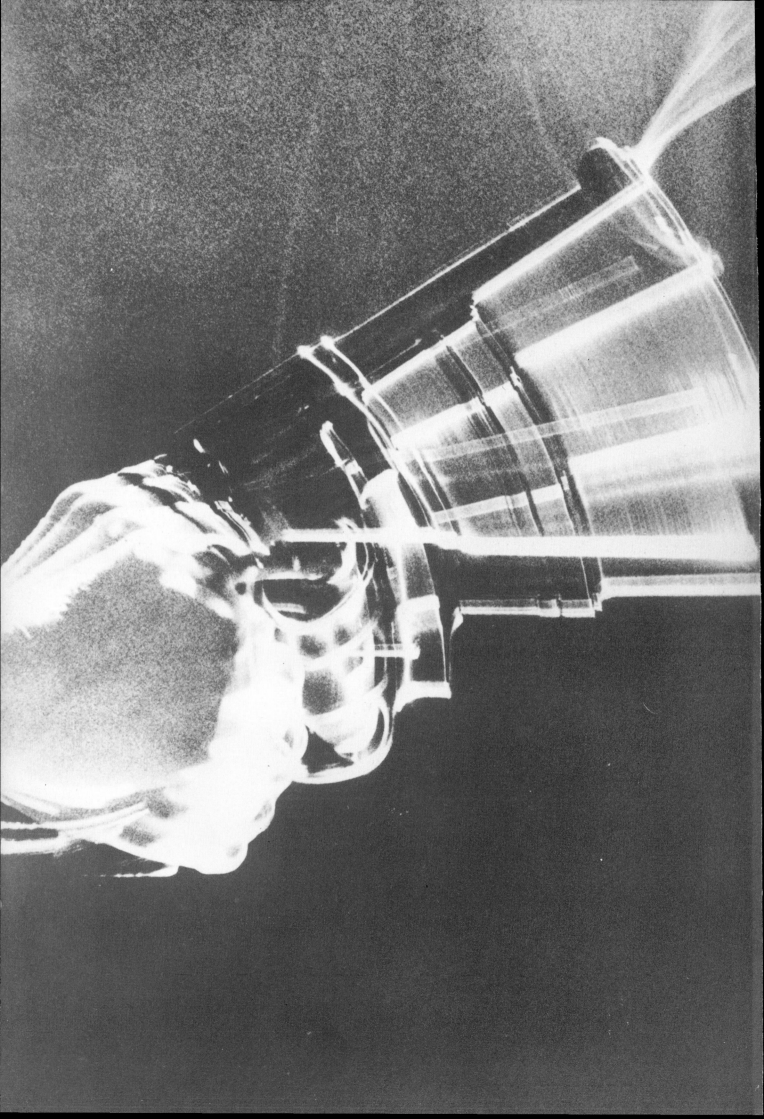